The Library Media Specialist in the Writing Process

Marge Cox

Carl A. Harvey II

Susan E. Page

Professional Development Resources for K-12
Library Media and Technology Specialists

Permission granted to reprint
Big6 Research Process © 2001 Michael Eisenberg and Robert Berkowitz
Information Search © 2005 Carol Kuhlthau
Kids Connect Toolbox © 2002 American Library Association
Savvy Seven © 2005 Nancy Miller and Connie Champlin
William and Mary Research Model © 2004 Center for Gifted Education
8 Ws of Information Inquiry © 1990 Annette Lamb
Quote from The Abracadabra Kid by Sid Fleischman © 1996.
Quote from How I Came to Be a Writer by Phyllis Reynolds Naylor © 1987

Library of Congress Cataloging-in-Publication Data

Cox, Marge.
  The library media specialist in the writing process / Marge Cox, Carl A. Harvey II, Susan E. Page.
    p. cm.
  Includes bibliographical references and index.
  ISBN 1-58683-214-X (pbk.)
  1. English language—Composition and exercises—Study and teaching (Elementary) 2. English language—Composition and exercises—Study and teaching (Secondary) 3. School librarians. I. Harvey, Carl A. II. Page, Susan E. III. Title.
  LB1576.C756 2007
  808'.042071—dc22

                                                        2006031502

Published by Linworth Publishing, Inc.
480 East Wilson Bridge Road, Suite L
Worthington, Ohio 43085

Copyright © 2007 by Linworth Publishing, Inc.

All rights reserved. Purchasing this book entitles a librarian to reproduce activity sheets for use in the library within a school or entitles a teacher to reproduce activity sheets for single classroom use within a school. Other portions of the book (up to 15 pages) may be copied for staff development purposes within a single school. Standard citation information should appear on each page. The reproduction of any part of this book for an entire school or school system or for commercial use is strictly prohibited. No part of this book may be electronically reproduced, transmitted, or recorded without written permission from the publisher.

ISBN: 1-58683-214-X

5 4 3 2 1

Table of Contents

Table of Figures 7
About the Authors 8
Introduction 10

Chapter 1: Research Important to Teaching Writing 13
    Teaching Writing as a Process 13
    The Product Approach 13
    The Process Approach 14
    Effective Strategies in a Process Approach 15
        Maximize the Reading and Writing Relationship 16
        Empower Students to Make Decisions. 16
        Teach Language Conventions in the Context of Writing 17
        Directly Teach the Major Modes of Writing. 17
        Teach Traits, Strategies, and Skills in Short, Focus Lessons 17
        Provide Immediate, Positive, Specific Feedback 18
        Engage Students in Identifying the Qualities of Effective Writing 18
        Use Writing across the Curriculum. 19
        Use Available Technology throughout the Writing Process. 19
    One More Thing… 19
    Ten Easy Ways to Share Information with Teachers 20
    Ten Easy Ways to Use Writing Across the Curriculum 20
    Works Consulted 21

Chapter 2: The Writing Process 23
    Understanding Terminology 23
    Writing Process 24
    Writing Traits 24
    Prewrite 25
    Draft 25
    Revision 25
    Editing. 26
    Publishing and Sharing 27
    Purposes for Writing 27
    Audience for Writing 28
    Types of Writing 28

    Collaborate with Teachers 29
    The Educator's Role in Prewriting. 29
    The Educator's Role in Drafting 31
    The Educator's Role in Revising. 32
    The Educator's Role in Editing. 33
    The Educator's Role in Publishing and Sharing. 33
    One More Thing… 34
    Works Consulted 35

Chapter 3: Collaboration 43
    First Steps in Collaboration. 44
    Instruction and Evaluation 44
    Provide Teacher Assistance. 45
    Provide Student Assistance. 47
    Provide Resources 47
    One More Thing... 48
    Works Consulted 48

Chapter 4: Prewrite 49
    Provide Teacher Assistance. 49
        Student Choice of Topic 49
        Prewriting Organization 50
    Provide Student Assistance. 51
        Prewrite Possibilities 51
        Think about the Audience. 52
        Know the Purpose. 52
        Get Focused 52
        Use Research Processes. 53
        Deliver a Message. 53
        Plan Organization 53
        Use Primary and Secondary Sources. 56
        Compile Sources 56
        Stay Focused 57
        Decide the Voice 58
    One More Thing… 58
    Literature Connections 58
    Works Consulted 59
    Sample Collaborative Lessons 60

Chapter 5: Drafting 65
    Provide Teacher Assistance. 65
        Encourage Drafts 65
    Provide Student Assistance. 65
        Model Drafting 65
        Discover and Maintain Focus. 67

    Use Anchor Papers 68
    Organize Writing 68
    Consider Adding More Information 69
    Coordinate Writing Products 71
  One More Thing… 71
  Literature Connections 71
  Works Consulted 72
  Sample Collaborative Lessons 73

Chapter 6: Revision 77
  Provide Teacher Assistance. 77
    Two Phases to Revision. 78
  Provide Student Assistance. 78
    Model Setting Priorities for Revision 78
    Share Revision Experiences and Tips from Other Writers 79
    Feature Writers in Your School. 79
    Share and Use Revision Checklists. 79
    Engage in Interactive Revision 80
    Hold Revision Mini-Conferences 80
    Revisit Familiar Strategies from Prewriting and Drafting. 81
    Provide Teachers with Professional Materials 81
  One More Thing… 82
  Works Consulted 82
  Sample Collaborative Lessons 83

Chapter 7: Editing 87
  Provide Teacher Assistance 87
  Provide Student Assistance. 88
    Choose Words Carefully 88
    Clarify Conventions. 88
    Correct Spelling 88
    Check Capitalization 89
    Organize Paragraphing 89
    Review Punctuation. 89
    Use Appropriate Grammar 90
    Apply Parts of Speech 90
    Examine Passive and Active Voice Verbs 90
    Eliminate Slang 91
    Cite Sources 91
    Offer Simple Solutions for Good Editing 92
  One More Thing… 92
  Literature Connections 92
  Works Consulted 94
  Sample Collaborative Lessons 96

Chapter 8: Publishing 101
    Options for Publishing 101
        Printing 101
        Speaking. 102
        Visual 102
        Web Opportunities 102
    Provide Teacher Assistance. 103
    Provide Student Assistance. 103
        Planning the Delivery and Presentation 104
    One More Thing... 104
    Literature Connections 104
    Works Consulted 105
    Sample Collaborative Lessons 106

Chapter 9: Response to Writing 111
    Informal Feedback 111
        Walking Feedback. 112
        Writing Conferences 113
        Written Feedback 113
        Interactive Technology 114
    Formal Evaluation 114
        Student Self-Evaluation 115
        Educators Evaluation 115
    One More Thing... 116
    Works Consulted 116

Glossary of Terms 117
Index. 119

Table of Figures

Figure 2.1	Modes of Writing	30
Figure 2.2	Prewrite	37
Figure 2.3	Draft	38
Figure 2.4	Revise	39
Figure 2.5	Edit	40
Figure 2.6	Publish	41
Figure 3.1	Collaboration Planning & Teaching Log	46
Figure 4.1	Research Process Samples	54
Figure 4.2	LP Ideas Web	60
Figure 4.3	LP Sources Cited	61
Figure 4.4	LP Note-Taking	62
Figure 4.5	LP Accepting-Rejecting Sources	63
Figure 5.1	Organizational Structures	70
Figure 5.2	LP Name That Character	73
Figure 5.3	LP If Then	74
Figure 5.4	LP Organization	75
Figure 5.5	LP Memory Mining	76
Figure 6.1	LP Picture It	83
Figure 6.2	LP Great Beginnings	84
Figure 6.3	LP Student Voice	85
Figure 6.4	LP Character Revisions	86
Figure 7.1	LP Spelling Word Walls	96
Figure 7.2	LP Parts of Speech	97
Figure 7.3	LP Active-Passive Voice	98
Figure 7.4	LP Connecting Language to the Time Period	99
Figure 8.1	LP Drawing	106
Figure 8.2	LP Brochures	107
Figure 8.3	LP Scripting	108
Figure 8.4	LP Web Page	109

About the Authors

Marge Cox

Marge's educational experience began as a classroom teacher. After several years there, she returned to college to get a Masters of Library Science and has spent the majority of her professional career focusing on integrating library media and classroom experiences. Marge also wrote a weekly book review column for 16 years that appeared in the local newspaper and taught library science and literature classes as adjunct faculty for Ball State University. Her commitment to professional growth includes membership and leadership roles in the Indiana State Reading Association, Association for Indiana Media Educators, and the Indiana Library Federation. Her love for literature, writing, and education provides the basis for her focus on the writing process for students and staff.

Carl A. Harvey II

Carl is the library media specialist at North Elementary School in Noblesville, Indiana. He has been active in the Association for Indiana Media Educators serving in various roles including Conference Chair, Young Hoosier Book Award General Chair, Survivor Workshop Chair, and President. For the Indiana Library Federation, he has served on various committees and will be President in 2008. He is also active in the American Association of School Librarians (AASL) and is currently the Chair of the Affiliate Assembly, co-chair for the 2007 National Conference in Reno, Nevada, and a member of the Advocacy Committee. He has published several articles in various professional journals including *School Library Journal, Library Media Connection, School Library Media Activities Monthly,* and *Teacher-Librarian.* The library media program at North was one of the first to receive a new distinction in Indiana—The Blue Ribbon for Exemplary School Media Programs. He also works part-time at the Speedway Public Library in Speedway, Indiana.

Dr. Susan E. Page

Susan's teaching experience spans elementary and secondary students in general and special education. Beginning in 1986, she began writing professionally about teaching, while continuing to provide staff development to educators. Across the years her focus has been on creating the conditions where students are active, successful participants in their own literacy learning. Susan believes that the writing process students are taught and use throughout the day is crucial to higher levels of engagement, understanding, and thinking. As she works with teachers and library media specialists, Susan witnesses the collective power of joining forces to establish writing as a tool students value and use effectively.

Acknowledgement

We would like to thank our families who have supported us during our own journey in the writing process, Karen Satterlee and Beth Schulte for their help and expertise in revising and editing our manuscript, and all the wonderful folks at Linworth Publishing for their support, encouragement, and guidance. Donald Murray has contributed significantly to our understanding and passion for writing. Thank you, Dr. Murray, for your many books, especially *A Writer Teaches Writing* and *The Craft of Revision*.

Introduction

Who will write the next generation of children's and young adult literature? Will there be others such as Richard Peck, Eve Bunting, or Christopher Paolini? Future writers for both children and adults sit in today's American classrooms and library media centers. Whether or not they go on to professional publication, today's job market demands that workers communicate effectively using the written word. Standardized tests and college entrance exams include required writing portions that students must pass. More than ever, schools put a larger emphasis on developing students and writers. The demand to develop student writing provides library media specialists with another opportunity to collaborate with teachers. Our experiences tend to center around the research process, but we can have an impact on the writing process as well. Taking advantage of the opportunity to help students become better writers can be another way to help us be indispensable in our schools.

In the pages that follow, we intend to provide you with an introduction to and understanding of the writing process. Just as we have worked for years to provide students with a process for research and how to look for and use information, there is also a process for writing to organize and use their thoughts, ideas, and all the information we have helped them to discover.

Depending on the level of collaboration in the building between you and classroom teachers, the amount of writing you may see or be involved with will vary. Our hope is that we can provide you with some sparks to help encourage collaboration centered on writing in your school.

For each step of the writing process, we have included sample lessons and collaboration connections where teachers and library media specialists can work together. We have divided our examples into grade designations of K-1, 2-5, 6-8, and 9-12. Defining levels is always subjective— you know your students better than we do. Our intention is for you to modify and adapt our examples for what will work best for you, your teachers, and your students.

By better understanding how writing should be taught and the kinds of support that are most helpful in moving from a blank paper to a finished piece, we will give needed and productive assistance to students and teachers. Just as you work with others, this book comes from collaboration among three educators with different perspectives: Marge is a former classroom teacher and currently a media services director at the district level; Carl is a library media specialist; Susan is a former classroom teacher who provides staff development in the writing process. Throughout this book we will share our experiences with you, designated by our first names.

We know that in some cases you have selected this book because you believe you lack sufficient knowledge of the writing process, and your school has started to emphasize writing. At the opposite extreme, you may have selected our book because your school works actively to improve students' writing, and knows best practices and works hard to implement them. Remember your professional life may change over time, too. At one point in her life, Marge provided professional library media services to seven elementary school libraries with clerks at each site. The teachers were totally product-driven when they taught writing. Was she able to co-teach writing with every teacher in each school? No! However, she started writing centers in the schools that were willing to have them. She included a writing instruction option in her monthly instruction to students. She taught the writing process during summer school. Was it a perfect scenario? No, but sometimes you just have to start with what you can do. To that end, we spent many hours discussing you, your needs, and how to provide the resources for today's situation with an eye on the future.

As a result of all the possibilities, you will notice that some of our guidance may feel out of your comfort zone: sharing information with teachers, expanding their understanding of the importance of student choice of topic, revision before editing, and conferencing with students. In some cases this may be just the type of information you need. If some of the best practices seem light years away from your current situation, take from our ideas those that have highest utility for you right now. We do not expect you to boldly go where no library media specialist has gone before, but we are convinced that your influence as a library media specialist is considerable and opportunities are abundant for improving the teaching of writing.

Chapters One and Two lay the groundwork for this book. These chapters delve into the research done on how best to teach writing, and the chapters provide an overview of the writing process. Chapter Three describes where the role of the library media specialist fits in this process, and it talks about collaborative opportunities for instruction. Chapters Four through Eight offer an in-depth look at each of the steps in the writing process, and provide specific connections for library media specialists. Sample collaborative lesson plans are supplied at the end of each chapter as well as a bibliography of recommended resources for educators and literature connections for use with students. The last chapter deals with assessment of student writing and potential roles the library media specialist might play in evaluation.

One last housekeeping issue before we get started. We decided to refer to "she" instead of "he/she" throughout the book when referring to library media specialists. This is no slight to male library media specialist—including our co-author. However, let's face it, the women outnumber the men in the library media specialist field! In an attempt to balance the scale, we use the pronoun, he, when referring to students.

Writing transcends all content areas. Library media specialists who understand how to teach writing can be valuable assets to other content areas as teachers incorporate writing into subjects other than language arts. Writing provides one more way for library media specialists and teachers to work together to help students achieve—the primary role of everyone in today's schools.

Chapter *1*

Research Important to Teaching Writing

As the library media specialist works with the students throughout the building, we see individual teachers take decidedly different approaches to learning. Some may be more project- and hands-on oriented. Others may assign more pencil and paper types of responses. While many factors may shape teachers' decision-making, their understanding of the research and best practices across and within disciplines are certainly key elements of the dynamics.

As a partner in developing and maintaining effective writing programs, you must know and understand the research on the teaching of writing. By being informed you will be able to increase your effectiveness as you provide resources, instruction, and insight about the writing process to students and their teachers.

It is wise to begin by writing more for your own purposes as you read this book and examine how the process works for you. In the chapters that follow, we will offer you many suggestions for helping teachers and for supporting students in writing for the intended audience and purpose. Some of what you do will impact the quality of a specific piece of writing. Ultimately, you have the possibility of positively influencing how the educators in your building view and teach students to use the writing process.

Teaching Writing as a Process

Prior to the 1980's there was debate about the most effective way to teach writing. Most of the debate centered on whether or not the product or the process approach was more effective. In the 1980's the debate largely ended with the process approach being clearly the winner (Cotton 3-4), despite the lack of controlled research studies and a wide range of variability within writing process approaches (Pritchard and Honeycutt 278-282). A greater understanding of both approaches is needed because the product approach is alive and well in many of today's classrooms.

The Product Approach

In the product approach, the teacher or instructor assigns a topic and gives the requirement of the task. The teacher is the principal, if not the sole, audience. The finished composition is given to the teacher. The teacher begins by marking each error in spelling, grammar, and punctuation. Once complete editing is finished, the teacher will make brief notes about organization or content with the remaining energy and time allocated to each paper. The draft may be the first and only version or students will be told to fix the mistakes and resubmit a "clean" copy. In most cases the teacher's feedback is given to the writer at the same time as the final grade. In the upcoming days and weeks, the teacher will give renewed energy to the convention errors that surfaced in the writing through a series of daily language skill exercises.

While there is a lack of research support for the product approach, it not only persists, but it is prevalent in schools for a number of reasons, including comfort, inertia, and lack of knowledge about how writing should be taught. Susan remembers vividly the rhythm of "correcting" student writing. She used a green pen because it seemed kinder than the red pen she experienced in school. While time consuming, she would go through each piece of writing sentence by sentence and mark each offending element. At the conclusion of her review, she would know she was done and would have something concrete for the students to do to improve their writing. While she was aware that the pieces usually sounded rambling and unfocused, Susan did not quite know what to do about that. Like many teachers, she had only one language arts course that touched on writing. During that phase of the course, the instructor offered fun activities for publishing writing, not strategies for teaching students how to write.

In contrast to the product approach, the teaching of the writing process has been found to consistently benefit student achievement in writing in correlational and experimental studies.

The process approach is based on the belief that successful writers go through the following identifiable stages to move from a blank paper to a published piece for the intended audience:

- Prewrite
- Draft
- Revise
- Edit
- Share/Publish

The five stages of the process are not linear, one following the other, but recursive. Depending on the writer, he may move from drafting back to prewriting and again onto drafting, or he might decide to abandon the topic for another one that the writer thinks has more promise.

The Process Approach

In the writing process approach, the focus of the writer is on communicating with the intended audience. Greater attention is given to the writer's topic, message, and delivery from prewrite through drafting and revision. Once the purpose for writing has been accomplished, the writer turns to the language conventions during editing.

Unlike the product approach, the teacher shows students how to act like successful writers. Lessons often begin with modeling of an important strategy, skill, or habit. The teacher may use his own writing or examples from other writers, including literature. As the lesson progresses, the teacher prompts and guides the students in applying new learning, including language conventions, in their own writing. Once mastered, the strategy, skill, or habit is integrated into existing knowledge to accomplish the writer's goals or to solve problems.

In the process approach, students will usually revise their writing by making notations and changes on the first draft. Recopying is reserved for publishing. Revision allows the writer to rethink the content message and make the changes he deems important to enhance meaning for the reader. As we will see in Chapter Five, revision is the heart of the writing process and an area where many teachers struggle with students' reluctance to revise or their tendency to put on "rose-colored" glasses when looking for changes that need to be made. To facilitate revision and editing, the teacher will often find time for conferencing and peer feedback.

A final major distinction between product and process approach is the amount of instructional time given to writing and the time allocated for students to write during class. Product approaches use much more of the class time for the practicing of isolated skills. The writing time is accomplished through homework. The process approach results in significantly more time devoted to writing instruction and sustained time to write during the instructional day. Depending on the teacher and the age of the students, process teachers may spend four to five more hours a week providing writing instruction and connected writing time. The writing process approach is described more fully in the chapters that follow.

In 1998, The National Assessment of Educational Progress (NAEP) reported a positive correlation between students' writing scores and the instructional practices at their schools. Practices included planning the writing, making an outline of some type, identifying the audience and purpose, and writing more than one draft. Students in all of the grades tested—four, eight, and twelve—scored significantly higher if they engaged in any type of prewriting when compared to those students who did not (Greenwald 103-104). One word of caution is needed. While there is correlational research to suggest the effectiveness of the writing process approach, some of the positive effects can be attributed to the increased instructional time mentioned earlier in this section.

According to the 1998 NAEP, most students in grades four, eight, and twelve are able to write at the basic level. The writing is generally organized, is understandable, includes some details, and the language conventions are generally intact so as not to prevent the reader from understanding the writer's meaning. In grades four and eight, 84 percent of the students tested scored at or above the basic level. In grade twelve, 78 percent of the writing was at or above the basic level. Regrettably, less than 30 percent of the students were able to write at the proficient level: 23 percent in grade four; 27 percent in grade eight; and 22 percent in grade twelve. Only one percent of the students scored at the advanced level. Most students were unable to create pieces that were "precise, engaging and coherent" (Greenwald 16).

Effective Strategies in a Process Approach

As you work with teachers, you will have the opportunity to learn from each other. The following research-based strategies will lead to more effective collaboration.

Maximize the Reading and Writing Relationship

In addition to increasing the amount of time devoted to writing instruction, using the reciprocal nature of reading and writing leads to higher levels of writing ability as well as reading ability. Students who are taught to read like a writer and to think like their reader as they are writing are sensitive to the use and underlying structure and patterns of our language. As writers, students can use what they know about reading to solve some of the problems in writing. When writing of any type is incorporated into content study, the result is higher levels of learning than when compared to activities that only involve reading and study (Langer and Applebee 135).

Teachers and media specialists increase students' awareness of the reciprocal relationship and its advantages for writers by using narrative and expository text during instruction. When teaching students how a type of writing, such as a personal narrative, is organized and developed, it is very helpful to share models from reading. Students who struggle with effective introductions and conclusions can examine reading materials to analyze how other authors crafted them. Precision in technical writing is enhanced after students try to follow the directions from a poorly written set of instructions from craft kits or recipes. When teaching specific traits, such as voice and fluency, it is powerful for students to sort samples in terms of quality and discuss why a particular author makes a better connection with them as the reader by applying skilled use of the trait in question.

Empower Students to Make Decisions

Harris and Graham have studied the self-regulated writer. Across the grades and curriculum, there is a noticeable difference in how students work as writers when they have been taught to think and make decisions. The use of a Writing Workshop format is a typical example of teaching students to take control of the writing process. The workshop usually begins with the teacher sharing information that will benefit the writer during the writing process. Sustained time to write follows with the teacher prompting and questioning students to examine their thinking and writing as they move through prewriting to drafting and revision (Lewis and Woodruff 3-7).

During the prewriting stage, students should select their topics, instead of relying on the teacher to suggest or assign them. Teachers who assign topics are quick to point out that the students are unable or unwilling to take that responsibility. However, in our experience, those same teachers have seldom had students construct a list of topics that represents what they know, care about, and have experienced. In content response writing, to explore or demonstrate understanding in social studies and mathematics, topics may be assigned, but students can narrow their topic or choose a point of view.

Teachers and library media specialists that recognize the importance of student ownership and judgment provide the writers with tools to increase their independence and effectiveness. Sample papers, revision and editing checklists, peer and teacher conferencing, and self-evaluation are all examples of fostering decision-making. Skilled questioning by teachers to cause students to reflect on the content and structure of their work are characteristic of classrooms where students make sound decisions.

Teach Language Conventions in the Context of Writing

Research continually highlights the lack of transfer to writing when grammar is taught in separate exercises, divorced from application in students' writing (National Writing Project and Nagin 22). Effective instruction in language skills is based on the errors students are making in their daily writing or the type of writing they are using. Contextualized instruction helps writers see the value and application of conventions. If students' drafts are filled with run-ons, focusing lessons on finding and fixing them will be valuable during the editing stage. When students are writing stories and personal narrative, it makes sense to teach the conventions for writing dialogue.

Sentence combining or teaching ways to embed one sentence within another of related meaning teaches students specific strategies to enhance meaning. Young writers, and those who struggle, benefit the most by learning to convert short, choppy sentences to longer ones. The result is writing that is more fluent and includes a variety of sentence patterns.

Directly Teach the Major Modes of Writing

Students benefit from understanding the purposes, organization, and structure of different modes and genres of writing (Donovan and Smolkin 140). Knowing, for example, that a compare and contrast composition is organized around two topics that are easily confused with each other, helps students pick appropriate topics. Further, understanding that the comparison can be organized around significant attributes paves the way for a productive prewrite.

Within the narrative, expository, and persuasive modes of writing, different formats reflect specific purposes or organization. For example, genres for narrative writing include personal narratives, short stories, mysteries, and fairy tales. Expository writing encompasses research reports, compare and contrast essays, and technical writing. As students move across the grades, they benefit from instruction that allows them to write for different purposes and to adapt the form of writing to their purpose and audience. Stated simply, Bill Peet found it more effective to bring his message about the environment to children in the form of a fairy tale, *The Wump World*, instead of a persuasive essay.

Teach Traits, Strategies, and Skills in Short, Focus Lessons

Brief lessons of 10 to 15 minutes can be useful to writers of all ages when they relate to the type of text they are constructing and the problems they face. These focus or mini-lessons have one clear teaching point, begin with direct explanation, and include modeling the use of the trait, skill, or strategy to improve the writer's message. Instruction time includes opportunities to try out the skill in the current piece, to raise questions, view the results, and receive the necessary support from the teacher (Hillocks 22-23). Using the format of a focus lesson, young writers quickly see that details can be added to the end of sentences to make them longer and more interesting. Mature writers readily grasp the concept of foreshadowing and try it out in their current piece. Students are much more receptive to learning the format of a bibliography when they are in the middle of a research report.

Individual or small group writing conferences with the teacher are another form of engaged, focused writing instruction. In a more personal context, students have time to seek assistance, ask questions, and discuss the problems they face as writers. Most conversations about writing occur during revision and editing, but can be used throughout the process. Properly conducted, students emerge from the conference with renewed energy and practical information to use immediately.

Provide Immediate, Positive, Specific Feedback

The most helpful and appreciated feedback is specific, positive, immediate, and given early and throughout the process (Dahl and Farnan 127-128). When these conditions are met and instructional strategies target the areas needed for improvement, writers feel energized and motivated to keep writing or write again. Specific feedback tells exactly what the reader found helpful, interesting, or meaningful in the piece. It may also address the writer's technique. "When I read the last part, I realized how hard it was for you to move to a new school." "Your writing sounds like music." "I can picture the tree house in your backyard." "Your introduction is informative and engaging."

The use of critical feedback should be kept to a minimum and preceded by specific and positive comments. When writers read or hear comments similar to the ones that follow, the writer is left with little hope and may be sorry he bothered to finish the work. "Your paper is filled with run-ons." "I was confused from the beginning to the end." "Did not anyone ever teach you how to use paragraphs?"

Feedback does not have to be limited to the teacher. Peer feedback consistently produces better writers and writing (Beach and Friedrich 225-231). Students can easily learn the type of feedback they should provide by thinking about the type they want as writers. When students are listening to each other's writing, they are not only working collaboratively, but also applying their knowledge of quality to content they find interesting—the life and ideas of their peers.

Engage Students in Identifying the Qualities of Effective Writing

Use of a rubric and sample or anchor papers are often the first step in defining quality. When teachers make explicit the characteristics that separate one paper from the rest, students think like writers and demonstrate higher levels of independence and competence than students who have not had the benefit of rubric training (Goodrich 14–17).

A companion to understanding quality is the use of formal criteria for students to self-evaluate their writing. The criteria should be given to students in advance of writing and the language of the rubric or checklist must be clearly understood. Self-evaluation of writing is correlated with higher motivation and competence of writers (Harris and Graham 162).

Use Writing across the Curriculum

"Thoughtful examination of ideas and opinions, of course, is a part of any good teaching" (Hillocks 214). Since writing is a tool for discovery, reflection, and thinking, its use across the curriculum and throughout the day is essential to make sense of the concepts and content in all disciplines. The theory that writing improves thinking is common sense and supported by research (Langer and Applebee 151).

Whether students are describing how they approached and solved a problem in mathematics, explaining the importance of inertia to skateboarding, or summarizing the impact of automation on the car industry, they are communicating their understanding of topics, content, and concepts at a level not possible with oral responses alone or in short answers to the teacher's questions. In addition, when teachers and library media specialists collaborate, writing occurs throughout the day. The result is higher retention and active rather than passive learning.

Use Available Technology throughout the Writing Process

Students' access to technology during the writing process often leads to superior writing when used in conjunction with instruction (MacArthur 259-260). Students, especially those who struggle, write more, especially in the middle school and high school when they are able to draft with word processors. The quality of the first drafts is generally better. Writers make more changes to their writing across drafts and when using word processors, the changes are more content related than when writing on paper. To take advantage of technology, students must know how to revise and how to type accurately and quickly (Troia 332).

In research funded by Microsoft, teachers spent less time on lecture and more time facilitating student learning when using laptops. Students made more decisions under these conditions. Not surprisingly, studies of the use of laptops report positive changes in student motivation and attitudes (Rockman 5).

One More Thing…

The research on the effectiveness of the writing process approach is extensive and helpful in knowing how to provide instruction, feedback, and support for writers. As you work with students and teachers, use the research to inform your decisions. Be aware of the numerous opportunities you have to change your practice in light of your knowledge about effective teaching strategies, and the conditions that bring out the best in writers. Share the knowledge with your teacher colleagues and begin or continue the dialogue about better ways of fine-tuning that will advance students' knowledge about writing and their enthusiasm for it. Listed below are many ways to begin the conversation. In the chapters that follow, we will explore the writing process in more detail.

Ten Easy Ways to Share Information with Teachers

1) Prepare a comparison chart of the characteristics of the product and process approaches. Share the chart in faculty meetings, and engage teachers in a discussion of why the process approach is superior for developing motivated, independent writers.

2) Provide displays of books and other print materials with an invitation to students to read like a writer. Discuss what that means and why it is helpful.

3) Use reflective questions to prompt rather than provide. Skilled questioning by adults fosters decision-making about what to do next, and it gives student writers confidence in their ability to solve problems.

4) Ask students to bring their writing folders or notebooks to the media center. Provide a few minutes occasionally for them to browse the shelves and add to their list, topics they know about and could share with others.

5) Be sure teachers see the opportunity to teach language skills along with editing. Model for them a lesson where students are taught sentence combining or the structure of paragraphs, and use the information immediately to edit their current piece.

6) Research your state standards and make a list of priority writing modes for each grade level. Share the information on a chart and point out how it can be used. Link this information to that of your standardized achievement data to heighten the importance of teaching writing.

7) Prepare PowerPoint slides on effective and ineffective feedback. Share them with the teachers and the students. Demonstrate effective feedback using student-writing samples.

8) Make a list for teachers of 10 Easy Ways to Use Writing across the Curriculum.

9) Demonstrate how to use technology with struggling writers to improve clarity and meaning. Application tools may allow teachers and writers to use a thesaurus, highlight of text, make comments, and even listen to it being read aloud by the computer.

10) Emphasize and reemphasize the crucial need for students to choose their own topics.

Ten Easy Ways to Use Writing Across the Curriculum

1) Use quick writes (sustained writing for two to three minutes) to identify what students already know about a topic or concept or to summarize important information from a discussion, experiment, or the viewing of media.

2) Use a graphic organizer or two-column notes to organize important information.

3) Have a discussion in class with one or more students writing about a topic while the teacher circulates.

4) Use exit or admit slips to have students summarize key ideas from the classwork or to begin the class by sharing three things they remember from the previous class.

5) Make a list of 10 important things about the topic.

6) Organize information in a list from least important to most important.

7) Write an analogy or comparison between what is being studied and the students' lives.

8) Write five questions about the topic after reading the introduction in the textbook or article.

9) Explain why or why not.

10) Describe an item or process and include how it works.

Works Consulted

Applebee, Arthur N. *Beyond the Lesson: Reconstructing Curriculum as a Domain for Culturally Significant Conversations.* Albany: National Research Center on Literature Teaching and Learning Report Series 1.7, 1993.

Beach, Richard, and Tom Friedrich. "Response to Writing." *Handbook of Writing Research. Ed.* Charles A. MacArthur, Steve Graham, and Jill Fitzgerald. New York: Guilford Publications, Inc., 2006. 248-262.

Bromley, Karen. "Key Components of Sound Writing Instruction." Best Practice: *Can Students Benefit from Process Writing Vol.1, No. 3*. Washington, DC: National Center for Education Statistics, April 1996. 152-174.

Cotton, Kathleen. *Teaching Composition: Research on Effective Practices.* School Improvement Research Series, Topical Synthesis #2. Portland: Northwest Regional Educational Laboratory, 2001.

Dahl, Karin L., and Nancy Farnan. *Children's Writing: Perspectives from Research.* Newark and Chicago: International Reading Association and National Reading Conference, 1998.

Donovan, Carol A., and Laura B. Smolkin. "Children's Understanding of Genre and Writing Development." *Handbook of Writing Research. Ed.* Charles A. MacArthur, Steve Graham, and Jill Fitzgerald. New York: Guilford Publications, Inc., 2006. 131-143.

Goldberg, Amie, Michael Russell, and Abigail Cook. "The Effect of Computers on Student Writing: A Meta-Analysis of Studies from 1992 to 2002." *The Journal of Technology, Learning, and Assessment* 2:1 (Feb. 2003): 3-51.

Goodrich, Heidi. "Understanding Rubrics." *Educational Leadership* 54:4 (Dec. 1996-Jan. 1997): 14-17.

Greenwald, Elissa A., et al. NAEP, 1998: *Writing Report Card for the Nation and the States.* Jessup: National Center for Education Statistics, 1999.

Hampton, Sally. "Strategies for Increasing Achievement in Writing." *Educating Everybody's Children: Diverse Teaching Strategies for Diverse Learners: What Research and Practice Say about Improving Achievement.* Ed. Robert Cole. Alexandria: ASCD, 1995.

Harris, Karen R., and Steve Graham. *Making the Writing Process Work: Strategies for Composition and Self-Regulation.* Cambridge: Brookline Books, 1996.

Hillocks, George. *Teaching Writing as Reflective Practice*. New York: Teachers College Press, 1995.

Langer, Judith, and Arthur Applebee. *How Writing Shapes Thinking: A Study of Teaching and Learning*. Urbana: National Council of Teachers of English, 1987.

Langer, Judith, and Sheila Flihan. *Writing and Reading Relationships: Constructivist Tasks in Writing Research/Theory/Practice*. Ed. R. Indrisano and James Squire. Newark: International Reading Association, 2000.

Lewis, Linda, and Elizabeth Woodworth. "Rituals, Routines and Artifacts: Classroom Management and the Writers Workshop." *America's Choice Writing Monograph Series*. Pittsburg: National Center on Education and the Economy, 2001.

National Writing Project, and Carl Nagin. *Because Writing Matters: Improving Student Writing in Our Schools*. 2nd ed. Indianapolis: Jossey-Bass, 2006.

The Neglected "R": The Need for a Writing Revolution. New York: The College Board, 2003.

Pritchard, Ruie J., and Ronald L. Honeycutt. "The Process Approach to Writing Instruction, Examining Its Effectiveness." *Handbook of Writing Research*. *Ed*. Charles A. MacArthur, Steve Graham, and Jill Fitzgerald. New York: Guilford Publications, Inc., 2006. 275-290.

Rockman Et Al. "A More Complex Picture: Laptop Use and Impact in the Context of Changing Home and School Access." *Executive Summary*. San Francisco: Rockman Et Al, 2004.

Sorenson, Sharon. *Encouraging Writing Achievement: Writing across the Curriculum*. Bloomington: Eric Clearing House on Reading and Communication Skills, 1991.

Troia, Gary A. "Writing Instruction for Students with Learning Disabilities." *Handbook of Writing Research*. *Ed*. Charles A. MacArthur, Steve Graham, and Jill Fitzgerald. New York: Guilford Publications, Inc., 2006. 324-336.

Urquhart, Vicki, and Monette McIver. *Teaching Writing in the Content Areas*. Alexandria: ASCD, 2005.

U.S. Department of Education. *The Nation's Report Card: Writing 1998*. Washington: US Department of Education; Office of Education Research and Improvement, 1998.

U.S. Department of Education. *The Nation's Report Card: Writing 2002, NCES 2003–529*, by H. R. Persky, M. C. Daane, and Y. Jin. Washington, DC: Institute of Education Sciences; National Center for Education Statistics, 2003.

Zemelman, Steven, et al. *Best Practice: Today's Standards for Teaching and Learning in America's Schools*. Portsmouth: Heinemann, 2005.

Chapter 2

The Writing Process

> *The Writing Process includes the stages a writer progresses through to move from a blank piece of paper to a finished piece that will be shared with the intended audience to accomplish the writer's purpose.*

Understanding Terminology

As a library media specialist, you communicate with teachers and students throughout the day. As you support the writing process, be aware that there are different interpretations of the writing process and the terms associated with it. Imagine a conversation between a library media specialist and a fourth grade teacher with two different definitions of revision.

> LMS: "Your students are so excited about their writing project. Many have asked for help in finding additional sources for their topics. A few have said they are in the revision stage."
>
> Teacher: "Yes, I dread revision. It is so hard to get them to change their writing. They think the first draft is the last."
>
> LMS: "Do they have trouble knowing what to cut or what areas need more details or elaboration?"
>
> Teacher: "Neither. They still can not seem to write in complete sentences, not to mention paragraphing."

Obviously the library media specialist was referring to the act of changing the ideas in a piece and the fourth grade teacher was thinking about revision as correcting spelling and grammar, editing. In this chapter you will receive an overview of the writing process and the terms associated with it. As you read, be aware of your prior knowledge and whether or not our view of the process matches your existing experiences and understanding. At the conclusion of this chapter, there are suggestions for clarifying the approach for teaching writing and terminology within your building and in conversations with individual teachers and students.

Writing Process

Most language arts teachers and library media specialists are aware of and use the phrase *writing process*. Most state standards refer to the writing process as a process one uses to communicate ideas with meaning and clarity for a variety of purposes and audiences. However, educators differ in their understanding of the purposes for writing, what should happen in each stage, and how to teach and support the stages of the process: prewrite, draft, revise, edit, and publish.

Writing process refers to the stages professional writers' typically use to move from a blank piece of paper to a final product that is shared with the intended audience. Writers will move back and forth among the stages rather than proceed in a linear way. The moving in and out of the stages results in the process being recursive.

Writing Traits

Traits refer to specific qualities of the writer's composition. These include:

1. Ideas
2. Organization
3. Voice
4. Word choice
5. Fluency
6. Conventions

Currently the most common approaches are 6-Traits (Spandel 2004) or 6+1 Traits™ (NWREL 2004). The "+1" refers to the presentation of the finished piece. Please be aware that while we see trait analysis and instruction as support for the writing process, not all educators share our view. Those who promote *6-Traits or 6+1 Traits* may use them as an end in itself instead of in support of the writing process. Using trait analysis as the entire writing program may be the case in the school in which you work. If so, the students are often taught one trait at a time, practice its use, and have their writing analyzed according to strengths and needs, based on the traits. Often in these well-intentioned approaches, students are seldom allowed to write about what they know and care about, but they are given a wealth of assigned topics. The isolating of specific skills or qualities and teaching them in isolation of the process may remind you of what took place in many schools when phonics was taught in isolation. In those days phonics was taught at a separate time from reading. Children completed phonics workbooks that were not linked to the reading material or overall process of reading to construct meaning.

As you read the next chapters, please notice how the writing process refers to the stages a writer goes through and ways in which direct instruction of the writing traits is linked to the steps of the process. For example, an understanding of organization is important when students are planning their writing (prewrite) and when they are revising their writing. During the editing stage of the process, the writer addresses the conventions to make his piece easier to read by attending to correct spelling and sentence structure. Being aware of the relationship between the writing process and writing traits may help you see opportunities for advancing the understanding of others.

Prewrite

Writers begin by collecting their ideas. There are many forms of doing so and most writers use several ways to collect the information that will grow into coherent ideas. In *A Writer Teaches Writing,* Donald Murray, a Pulitzer Prize author and writing teacher, identifies six ways to collect ideas: awareness, observation, recall, empathy, interviewing, and research. To state it simply, writers draw on their experiences to write about what they know about and care about. They may also investigate a topic where they are interested and share what they learn.

A companion to the collection of ideas is the planning. Thinking about the topic or plot, the intended message, audience, and the focus of the writing begins during prewrite. The overall organization of the ideas the writer will develop is considered. When students are preparing to write in a format such as compare and contrast, the trait of organization may receive particular attention. Teachers may even specify that students arrange their ideas on a graphic organizer such as a T-chart or Venn diagram during the prewrite stage. At other times, the students may simply be expected to prewrite and may be given several options for doing so.

Therefore, prewriting may be observable by the writer making lists or organizing ideas on a planner such as a story map. Some writers prewrite by free writing for a period of time on paper without stopping. Other people may prewrite by thinking and planning in their head or rehearsing. Prewrite defines the topic, audience, focus, overall message, organization, and the writer's voice. It is not a blueprint that should be followed exactly to completion. Some of the information that appears on a list or organizer will not be used in the actual piece. Other information that is not a part of the prewrite may present itself on the paper during the drafting process. The ideas that pop into the writer's mind during writing are one example that writing is discovery. Prewriting may take place for a short period of time before the drafting begins, or it may go on for days!

Draft

As students begin to put their ideas onto paper, they are drafting. The goal of the writer is to let the writing flow to communicate information that the reader needs or will find interesting. Drafting is a sustained effort that continues as the piece is developed. Drafting results in a product that has a beginning, middle, and end. However the writer may pause, reread what is written, return to the prewrite stage to gather more information, or simply write non-stop. Successful writers are aware of the process and apply many of the traits and skills they have learned as they write. They choose ideas and words that will enable their reader to understand and be interested in their message. Proficient writers want the piece to sound like them: to have their voice, humor, enthusiasm, perspective, attitude, or tone.

Revision

Once the writer has created the whole, he rereads the piece, analyzing what needs to be done to make the ideas and information clearer and more meaningful to the reader. A simple way to distinguish revision from editing is that revision addresses how the writing *sounds*.

During revision, writers read and reread their pieces, multiple times until they have obtained the clarity and meaning they intended. The writer may ask several questions.

- Is my purpose clear? Is the underlying message clear?
- Was I focused on one thing?
- Were the reader's questions answered?
- Does this sound like me?
- What gaps are there?
- What might bother or confuse the reader?

Revision should proceed from whole to part and usually has two phases that are not distinct, but blended. At first, the writer decides whether the overall message and ideas are clear, what works, and what does not work. Changes may include moving information around, adding information, and deleting information. Revision is not done a line at a time in this first stage. During revision, we may see the writer move around from middle to end to beginning. Once stage one of revision has been accomplished, the writer may make more minor or subtle changes by substituting a more precise word or including an additional example. In the second phase of revision, students may go through their work a line at a time and even analyze it a trait at a time.

Revision is not always necessary. Sometimes the writing works well enough for the intended purpose and audience. For example, if a student is writing in preparation for posting on a blog the similarities and differences between two books on the same theme, revision may not be necessary. Much of the writing has probably already been revised in the writer's head during rehearsal and drafting.

Editing

In editing, the writer removes the obstacles that can distract from the intended message. These culprits include spelling, punctuation, capitalization, agreement (subject-verb, pronoun-antecedent) and structure of sentences and paragraphs.

In reality, editing, or changing how the writing looks, often takes place during revision. While revising this section, we returned to a sentence that needed a comma. However, editing needs to be a separate stage in the teaching of writing or novices will get distracted by spelling and punctuation from their goal of meaning and clarity. Once students start editing, they seldom find their way back to revision. The writing ends up looking great but sounding flat, lifeless, or disorganized.

Publishing and Sharing

Once the writing sounds and looks the way the writer thinks it should for the audience, it may be put in a more finished form and delivered to the audience. In school, publishing can take many forms. Sometimes publishing is simply a writer reading his piece to a small group of students interested in the topic. Publishing may include recopying the text or using a word processor to give a neater or more professional presentation. Publishing may also mean sending the writing off to a contest sponsored by members of the community to address a topic or cause important to the group.

Once published, the writing process has concluded. Usually there is a deep sigh of relief and celebration at what has been communicated and accomplished. Typically the longer the process has been from planning to publication, the greater the joy!

Unfortunately, what we have just described is not the reality in many classrooms and schools. The reason is simple. Many teachers and library media specialists did not receive an in-depth understanding of the writing process in their coursework. Further, their experiences as students in school were quite different than those just described. One of the teachers in a recent workshop shared the following comments on how the process works in his classroom:

"So that is what the writing process is supposed to be! Well, in my classroom, it works a little differently. I give them a topic, the students groan. Then I show them how to prewrite by making a cluster on the overhead to plan out the writing. Some of my students participate and suggest ideas. Then I tell them it is time to write. Many of my students sit there as I circulate and say they can not think of anything to write about. Patiently I keep redirecting them to the plan 'we' created. After one or more days, most students finish their drafts. A few do not seem to finish anything. Then I tell them it is time to revise. Even after I show them how I would revise my piece most students sit there and change very little. What they do change is really an edit. Then I conference with students by having them bring their writing to me one at a time. I ask them what they think needs to be changed. Many students tell me they do not think anything needs to be changed. I then work through their piece a paragraph at a time, making suggestions. This takes at least 15 minutes per student and goes on for days. By the time the students are 'ready' to edit I am worn out, and most writing has not been changed very much at all. We edit and publish writing that is a little better, but not much, and then it is time to do it again."

During his description, there was much head nodding and smiling by his colleagues in the workshop. A few elaborated on his ideas or mentioned difficulties with time or motivation by students.

Purposes for Writing

While there are identifiable stages to writing, the process varies greatly according to style, personality, experience, and the purpose for writing. Generally, there are three main reasons to write: (1) to communicate ideas with someone across space and time, (2) to explore one's understanding or beliefs about a subject, and (3) to demonstrate understanding about a topic or to prove competence.

The first purpose, communicating ideas, is most prominent in national standards. This type of writing can be anything from writing a letter to a friend to a personal narrative to technical writing of job-related documents. The final product is given to the intended audience or "published" when the writer feels it has accomplished its purpose. Publishing can be anything from dropping a letter in the mailbox to sending off a piece to a writing contest.

When using writing for the second purpose, thinking and discovery, the writer may explore his thinking about the topic with a list, quick write, or a summary to reveal his thinking, perspective, and understanding. Writing for discovery can also be the start of framing purposes and questions for an inquiry or investigation. This type of writing usually stays with the writer but may lead to a more formal piece later. Many writing experts point out that all writing is discovery (Murray 51-52). While this is true, as a library media specialist, you will want to offer different strategies and tools when students are writing primarily for communication than when they are using writing to explore their knowledge and understanding.

Writing can also be used to demonstrate competence and understanding of a topic or area of study. The audience for this type of writing is usually someone who is an expert in a discipline or field of activity. When the writer feels he sounds competent or has proven the understanding needed for a job, course, or assignment, the writing is given to the audience. Writing to demonstrate competence or understanding may go through several drafts and revisions or may be a single first draft.

Most often the type of writing you support will fall into the first category. Students will typically be asked to share their ideas with a limited audience. Most of the time, students' writing will be published by turning it in for feedback and a grade. In Chapter Eight, you will receive several great ideas for expanding students' and teachers' concepts about publishing and writing for people beyond their families and classmates.

Audience for Writing

Audience is central to the writing process. How a writer approaches a topic and what is said depends upon the audience for the piece. Recently, Susan was catching up on e-mails and wrote about the stray kitten that had wormed its way into her home. To the first friend, a cat lover, she used two paragraphs to detail the cuteness of the kitten's antics. To the other friend, she covered the information about the kitten in two sentences.

As a library media specialist, being aware of the importance of audience will help you decide what type of assistance is needed by students and when you can expand teachers' thinking about the assignments and projects they use. For example, when a student says she is writing about frogs, ask who the audience is. If she says her classmates, then you can help the writer consider what the readers already know and what might be interesting and new information. If the audience is the teacher, then ask if the assignment specified the purpose and the type of writing.

Types of Writing

The writing that students do falls into one of three categories, and can be classified under four domains or types: expository, persuasive, narrative, and poetry. Expository writing attempts to explain, inform, and address one or more topics or concepts. Persuasive writing addresses one or more topics as well, but the focus of the writer is convincing the audience or motivating the reader to action. Narrative writing is designed to tell a story and may take many forms including personal narrative and science fiction. Poetry also has many forms, but its primary purpose is to express ideas, inspire, or entertain. Within each domain, there are norms or conventions for the format or organization of the writing.

Collaborate with Teachers

As mentioned earlier in this chapter, many teachers lament the fact that they were ill-prepared to teach writing based on their experiences or the knowledge they gained in college. When teachers admit this during workshops and conversations, they also frequently confess that they have not ever read a book on the teaching of writing by recognized experts (Donald Murray, Donald Graves, or Lucy Calkins), or it has been a l-o-n-g time since they did.

Therefore, do not be surprised if you encounter wonderful teachers who demonstrate one or more of the ineffective practices listed in the next section. Your role is not to change teachers but to work with them. Being aware of the approach individuals are using will help you provide the type of support that is appropriate for their students' situation. You may also find that in addition to helping teachers help their students, you can be a change agent by tactfully sharing some of the information you glean here and from the recommended readings in the bibliography. Beginning in the next chapter, you will find many specific suggestions for your role in supporting each stage of the writing process.

The Educator's Role in Prewriting

Since prewriting involves the collection of ideas and planning, wise teachers have laid the foundation necessary to avoid the writer's helpless look, followed by the dreaded words, "I can not think of anything to write about." One important thing a teacher will do to avoid difficulties at the start is to first engage the students in discovering and making a list of possible topics and audiences for their writing. By exploring what they know about, care about, have experienced, and are interested in, writers have a starting point. Second, if the teacher has taught the students several different ways to explore their ideas, prewriting usually goes smoothly. Writers will move to drafting with a good idea about their topic, focus, organization, and needs of their audience.

Helpful Teaching

- Organize writers with a notebook or folder that can go wherever they go with their list of individual topics and other writer's tools.
- Show students various forms of prewriting that includes "sitting and thinking," brainstorming with a cluster or list, talking with a friend, and quick writes. Include technology applications, such as Kidspiration/Inspiration in the demonstrations.
- Let students share with each other types of prewriting that work for them.
- Provide demonstrations of how to narrow the topic and consider the wants and needs of the audience.

Figure 2.1 Modes of Writing

Mode	Purpose	Examples of Final Products
Expository	To inform or to explain	Chart Report/Research papers Essay Manual Procedures
Persuasive	Convince of a certain point of view or to motivate to action	Letter to the editor Essay Critique Project proposal Letter of complaint Debate
Narrative (fiction or nonfiction)	Recount: to tell what happened	Personal narrative Anecdote Biography Journal Short story Novel
Poetry	Express ideas, inspire, entertain	Blank verse Cinquain Free verse Haiku Rhymes

Counter-Productive

- Doing the work for students, including suggesting their topic or prewriting for them. Once the students have been shown how to do something, switch from modeling to prompting and guiding to requiring students do the work, O.T.O. (On Their Own) before any assistance is given.
- Giving the impression that there is only one way to prewrite.
- Seeing prewrite organizers as blueprints and saying, "Unless it is on your planner, you cannot include it."

Special Considerations for Prompted Writing and Assignments

- Even when students are writing for formal assessment with a writing prompt, they can still narrow the topic to give themselves an advantage. For example, if students are told to write to explain what career is best suited for them and fluctuate between being a brain surgeon and a teacher, have them think about which one they know more about and will result in specific examples and details for their audience.
- Teach students that restating the question or prompt when writing for assessment purposes helps make their focus clear.
- If students are conducting research, require that they organize notes around specific inquiry questions.

The Educator's Role in Drafting

During drafting, some students will struggle with just beginning. Give them suggestions for getting three lines down, such as beginning to write why it is difficult to begin to write. Remind writers to freely write their ideas and not to be concerned with good writing.

Helpful Teaching

- Model for students how to get started.
- Remind students to write on every other line, or set the computer to double space, so there is room to make revisions when working from a printed copy.
- Circulate as students draft. Encourage, but do not linger.
- Establish a common time for students to write everyday so they come in thinking like writers.
- Give strategies for continuing to write, including setting goals of how much they will write before they pause or look at the clock.

The Educator's Role in Revising

Once the first draft is completed, wise teachers show the students how to rethink or re-see their writing through the eyes of the reader. The concept is best demonstrated by having students listen to the writing of others, including the teacher's, to give specific compliments first: "What did you notice or appreciate as a reader?" Next ask the students to listen again to determine the message, theme, or plot (narrative). If there does not appear to be one, then revision has begun. If there is, then ask students if there is anything that is unclear or confusing about the piece. Once the piece has passed through the first phase of revision, show how polishing can occur by making a few additions and substitutions or by deleting or rearranging information.

Helpful Teaching

- Show students how to listen to their writing by reading it softly and slowly (touching each word).
- Demonstrate how to use sticky notes and margins to add information or to reorganize their writing.
- Confer with students in small groups about their intended message and audience.
- Prompt the writer to discover what needs to be changed.
- Provide focused teaching in small groups for ways to solve common problems that have surfaced, such as writing an interesting beginning.

Counter-Productive

- Editing during revision.
- Having students rework the piece past reason in light of the purpose and audience.
- Telling the students what to change or suggesting how something could be reworded.

Special Considerations for Prompted Writing and Assignments

- In formal writing assessment, the writer should revisit the prompt to be sure he is writing for the "intended" audience, not the classroom teacher.
- When writing to demonstrate content knowledge, students should carefully attend to presenting accurate information and using precise content language. This may involve looking back into the texts and notes.

The Educator's Role in Editing

Since this stage involves making the piece easier to read by applying the necessary conventions, students may need direct teaching or prompting to do so. Some students will need more support than others. Most teachers find modeling and an editing checklist to be helpful tools.

Helpful Teaching

- Focus on having students apply one or two conventions from recent teaching.
- Prompt students rather than point out mistakes: "There is a problem with subject-verb agreement in this paragraph."
- Praise writers for what they do find and fix.

Counter-Productive

- Letting students line up at the teacher's desk to be told what to fix.
- Editing before revision.
- Over-editing (to perfection) when the purpose and audience does not warrant it.

Special Considerations for Prompted Writing and Assignments

- Know the guidelines and rubrics that will be used for formal writing assessment. Most tolerate a few mistakes, typical in first drafts. Generally the content (ideas) is much more important than the conventions.
- In content writing assignments, conventions play a minor role and are typically limited to legibility, spelling, capitalization, and sentence and paragraph structure.

The Educator's Role in Publishing and Sharing

Ideally, no change occurs at this point except those that affect presentation. The writer simply needs ideas, encouragement, and possibly supplies for presenting their writing to the audience.

Helpful Teaching

- Show students examples of several options for publishing.
- For more elaborate forms, such as book-making, provide written directions as well as modeling.

Counter-Productive

- Allowing students to publish work that has only been recopied, not revised for meaning and clarity.

- Publishing a piece of writing by making it attractive, but failing to have the writer deliver it to the audience and receive feedback.

One More Thing…

Writing is not a linear process, but a recursive one. During writing, ideas are collected, organized, and formed in light of the topic, purpose, audience, and message. The writer moves through predictable stages that begin with prewriting and end with publishing or sharing. However, there is no one way to write effectively, and the process works differently for each writer and each type of writing he produces.

Most writing has a central purpose of communicating ideas with an audience that wants or needs the information. Depending on the audience, the writing may also be a tool for discovery, inquiry, or to demonstrate competence and understanding of a topic or area of study. The structure of the writing may be expository, persuasive, narrative, or poetic. Within the modes there are multiple formats that include everything from lists of procedures to novels.

Writing for any purpose is a creative venture where the writer shapes ideas and transmits them in the clearest way possible so that the audience will understand the writer's message and find it interesting and relevant. The audience may be the writer himself or someone he has never met. The care with which the piece is drafted, revised, and edited relates to how the writing will be shared, as well as the audience. The media center houses a wealth of resources to support writers as they learn to use the process!

Teachers play a critical role in teaching students how to use the writing process for a variety of audiences and purposes. Their professional knowledge and judgment are critical to improving student writing for any purpose. Teachers can greatly impact students' motivation for writing through the instruction, experiences, and feedback they give to student writers.

Library media specialists have many opportunities to influence the quality of student writing as they collaborate with students and their teachers.

- Be aware that individual teachers may see and teach the writing process differently. Ask them how they typically use and manage the writing process from prewrite through publishing. Listen carefully as they talk about revision. If necessary, ask how revision differs from editing in their classroom. Clarify other terminology as needed as a continuing process of improving communication about and support of writing.

- Consider providing displays of the steps of the writing process in the library media center. Avoid commercial posters if possible. Instead develop posters that are created by a discussion among the staff and supported by research. These might be similar to those shown in Figures 2.2-2.6 on pages 37-41.

- Develop a glossary of writing terminology. Consider including definitions from the glossary on page 117, the posters on pages 37-41, and additional terms as you read this book. Update your glossary every few weeks with terms from your reading and that of your colleagues.

- Be aware of opportunities to build teacher knowledge about the writing process. Summarize the key findings of the research from Chapter 1. Organize a study group around the ideas in this chapter. Discuss how the writing process in the real world is similar or different to the one used in your school and classrooms.

In the next five chapters you will gain a more in-depth understanding of the writing process and receive many specific ideas you can use with students and teachers.

Works Consulted

Bauman, Amy, and Art Peterson. *Breakthroughs: Classroom Discoveries about Teaching Writing*. Washington: National Writing Project, 2002.

Burke, Jim. *Writing Reminders: Tools, Tips, and Techniques*. Portsmouth: Heinemann, 2003.

Caswell, Roger, and Brenda Mahler. *Strategies for Teaching Writing*. Alexandria: ASCD, 2004.

Dignan, Jennifer. *"Reality Grammar: Understanding Sentence Structure"* Literary Cavalcade Feb. 2005. 30 Sep. 2006 <teacher.scholastic.com/writeit/cavalcade/PDF/feb2005/reality_grammar_p20_22.pdf>.

Graves, Donald, and Penny Kittle. *Inside Writing: How to Teach the Details of Craft*. Portsmouth: Heinemann, 2005.

Kozlow, Michael, and Peter Bellamy. "Experimental Study on the Impact of the 6+1 Trait Writing Model on Student Achievement in Writing." Proc. of ... 2005 ASCD Annual Conference. Portland: Northwest Regional Educational Laboratory, 2004.

MacArthur, Charles, Steve Graham, and Jill Fitzgerald, editors. "The Effects of New Technologies on Writing and Writing Processes." *Handbook of Writing Research, Ed*. New York: Guilford Publications, Inc., 2006. 248-262

Murray, Donald M. *Write to Learn*. 8th ed. Belmont: Heinle/Thomson, 2004.

Murray, Donald M. *A Writer Teaches Writing*. Rev. 2nd ed. Belmont: Heinle/Thomson, 2004.

National Board for Professional Teaching Standards—Library Media Standards. 2001. National Board for Professional Teaching Standards. 30 Sep. 2006. <www.nbpts.org/pdf/ecya_lm_standards.pdf>.

National Standards: Language Arts. National Council of Teachers of English. 30 Sep. 2006. <www.education-world.com/standards/national/lang_arts/index.shtml>.

National Writing Project, and Carl Nagin. Because Writing Matters: Improving Student Writing in Our Schools. Rev ed. Indianapolis: Jossey-Bass, 2006.

Peet, Bill. *The Wump World*. Boston: Houghton Mifflin Company, 1981.

Spandel, Vicki. *Creating Writers through 6-Trait Writing Assessment and Instruction*. 4th ed. Upper Saddle River: Pearson Education, Inc., 2004.

Spandel, Vicki. *Creating Young Writers: Using the Six Traits to Enrich Writing Process in Primary Classrooms*. Upper Saddle River: Pearson Education, Inc., 2004.

Standards for the English Language Arts: A Joint Publication of NCTE and IRA. The National Council of Teachers of English. 30 Sep. 2006. <www.ncte.org/about/over/standards/110846.htm>.

Teachers: Write It. Scholastic Inc. 30 Sep. 2006. <teacher.scholastic.com/writeit/>.

Tompkins, Gail E. *Teaching Writing: Balancing Process and Product*. 4th ed. Upper Saddle River: Prentice Hall, 2003.

Figure 2.2   Prewrite

Prewrite

Get Ready to Write

■ Decide what your topic, audience, and purpose is likely to be.

■ Choose a method for exploring your topic, sorting our your ideas, thinking about your message or focus:

– Talk with someone

– Sit and think

– Make a list

– Use an organizer

– Free-write for several minutes

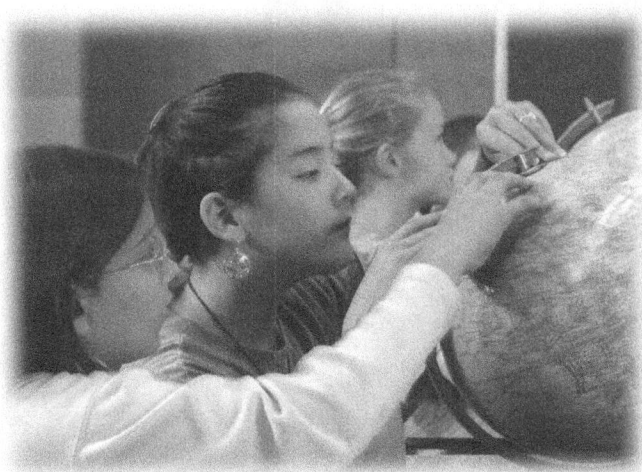

Figure 2.3   Draft

Draft

Write or Type Your Thoughts

- Write as continuously as possible.

- Keep focused on your audience and what you are trying to communicate.

- Pause occasionally, to think about how to say something or get your message across.

Figure 2.4   Revise

Revise

*Make Changes So that Your Writing
Is Easily Understood and Interesting*

■ Decide if your purpose and message are clear. What is the one thing you want your readers to know, understand, or believe about your topic?

■ Use the four revision tools to improve your ideas, organization, word choice, flow, and voice:
   —Add
   —Delete
   —Rearrange
   —Substitute

The Writing Process   *39*

Figure 2.5   Edit

Edit

Make the Writing Easy to Read

■ Check and change words that are misspelled.

■ Use correct format for sentences and paragraphs so your reader is not distracted.

■ Check for the other items on your editing checklist.

Figure 2.6 Publish

Publish

*Recopy, Print Out, and Make It
Attractive for Your Audience*

■ If you are going to read it to your audience, prepare so it flows and sounds like you.

■ Write legibly or type so that your reader can concentrate on the ideas you have written.

■ Use visuals and materials to make an attractive presentation.

Chapter 3

Collaboration

Traditionally, library media specialists provide resources for both students and teachers. In that role we have done everything from finding "that book that was my sister's favorite one" to locating the "perfect" Web site. Today our role has expanded to include more collaboration with teachers and instruction with students. We have many more opportunities to work with classroom teachers to plan instruction, teach lessons, and evaluate student work. By being an active participant, you have the opportunity to impact instruction in all curriculum areas, including writing. Chapters Four through Nine will provide specific examples of ways the library media specialist can be an active partner during each stage of the writing process. We will begin with the big picture of establishing a collaborative relationship with teaching partners, then deciding what should be taught, and planning for instruction.

While some teachers welcome your expertise and perspective, some teachers are accustomed to going it alone. Often the hardest part of working as a library media specialist is finding opportunities to collaborate with the classroom teacher. Territorial issues often abound in schools. Teachers find a way that works well for them, and they want to stick with it! As the library media specialist, you must capitalize on each new opportunity. All it may take is one great lesson or activity and the wall can begin to crumble down. In recent years, the standards movement has dictated that teachers self-examine what they are doing and be able to clearly demonstrate how their instruction is helping students achieve. Like it or not, standardized tests are the norm across the country. We, as library media specialists, must demonstrate how we can help our students' succeed on these tests.

For example, a group of fourth grade teachers were working on redoing their year-long plan. They were adjusting their themes and units to closely align with the state standards (which are the basis for the state test). Carl was there and joined in the discussion. Working together, they found connections and the collaboration evolved into a year-long collaboration to achieve integrated units that supported the state standards. In another situation, the teachers were working with a district coach on writing. The teachers were given a variety of strategies to use in their classrooms, but they still had questions. Carl seized the opportunity to find resources and suggested lessons he could co-teach, based on the coach's strategies. It is all about finding that opportunity and taking advantage of it.

Consider the opportunities to build collaborative bridges. Listen to conversations in the cafeteria. Be aware of what is happening in the building, and be proactive to make suggestions for possible collaborative experiences to teachers. Do not be shy or bashful. Social gatherings like staff parties and gatherings after school give teachers a chance to see you outside the school setting. When they realize you are a "real" person, then they will be more comfortable wanting to work with you collaboratively.

Finding that right first project can often be a tedious task. Many veteran teachers have long established projects they enjoy teaching, so starting there may not be the best idea. One strategy library media specialists might use with those veteran teachers is to look for those standards or curriculum topics that teachers do not enjoy. If the library media specialist can produce a project idea that will make teaching that material more enjoyable for the teacher and better for students, it may just provide that foot in the door that will lead to other collaborative experiences.

Beyond the ability to see collaborative opportunities, the library media specialist has to be aware of the standards and district requirements. You need to have the standards at ready access and be able to use them during planning sessions with teachers. While we all hope the classroom teacher is well versed in their standards, we also know that is not always the case. The library media specialist needs to work towards becoming as fluent with the standards as the teachers should be.

First Steps in Collaboration

By working together, a teacher and library media specialist can have a strong impact on the learning environment created for students. The preliminary discussion provides an opportunity for each to share ideas, strategies, and strengths they bring to the project. Two (or more) people working together can mask weaknesses in each other and build a superior learning opportunity for students. Schedules, especially at the elementary level where the library might be on a fixed schedule, may make this type of conversation more difficult. However, even in the fixed schedule environment, the opportunity to collaborate still exists. At the secondary level, the stumbling block may be the push to "cover content curriculum," but when experience demonstrates that collaboration saves time and positively impacts student achievement, secondary teachers are very receptive to collaboration.

Instruction and Evaluation

Sitting together to decide what you want students to learn and be able to do is a great starting point for the collaboration. A collaboration log is a wonderful tool for mapping out the planning process. See Figure 3.1 on page 46 for an example. Local school corporations may have developed specific curriculum guides to aid in your decision making. In addition, most states have written academic standards and indicators for each subject area and grade level.

Writing standards are generally located under English/language arts. Each state has tackled the role of library media program in various ways. Some have made them their own separate academic subject, some have no mention at all, and still others look for correlations between the Information Literacy Skills and the state academic standards. Logic dictates these standards would determine what students need to learn. Teachers and library media specialists creatively determine how to combine multiple standards in a variety of curriculum areas to have the biggest impact for students.

Taught in isolation, it would be impossible to meet all of the standards, but by grouping them into themes and units, teachers and library media specialists can efficiently and creatively teach the standards. No matter what subject area or grade level you are planning, writing is going to play a crucial part in instruction. If we look at the Information Literacy Standards, they focus on students using, creating, and generating knowledge. In doing all of that, students have to find effective means to communicate, which means at some point in that process they will be writing.

Once you and the teacher decide on what students should learn, instruction, projects, and activities can be developed to help reach those goals. First, determine the resources that will be needed to accomplish the project and activities—books, videos, magazines, and other instructional supplies. As the planning moves forward, the library media specialist and classroom teacher can begin to assign tasks. Whose job will it be to teach the mini-lesson on locating information in online databases? Whose job will it be to teach the students what elements are contained in a good biography? For successful endeavors, roles and responsibilities need to be clearly defined, including evaluation.

> **For links to the various state standards, you can go to <edstandards.org/Standards.html>**

Collaboration may also extend into evaluation and involve two separate aspects: evaluation of student understanding and evaluation of the project design and implementation. Before instruction begins, decide how student learning will be determined. Discuss with the teacher(s) what type(s) of evaluation you will use and what role you each have in the process. Assessing student attainment of goals may be something the teacher and library media specialist do together, or divide up. For example, the library media specialist may grade the research component and the teacher may grade the final product. Once student work has been evaluated, decide what instructional changes and resources could have led to higher levels of student performance.

Evaluation of design and implementation should begin in the planning stage with discussion of the benefits of collaboration for teachers and students. Your conversation will lead to a better understanding of your individual and mutual expectations and the working style of each. If the project is a long one you will want to discuss, "How is it going?" at checkpoints along the way. If the project will last two weeks or less, set a day and time to decide what worked and what did not. Talk about ways collaboration could be more effective. Explore changes that might improve the effectiveness of your collaboration the next time.

Provide Teacher Assistance

When Susan works with secondary and elementary teachers, many will admit they were not trained in the teaching of writing. Therefore, as you begin collaboration, do not be surprised if some of the most knowledgeable teachers are not as well grounded in writing research and best practices as you would have thought. Some teachers will welcome hearing about what you are reading and trying out new ideas with you. Others may feel "experience is the best teacher" and will be uncomfortable with implementing something new in front of a colleague. Consider carefully how to share your own emerging understandings and enthusiasm while keeping your working relationship intact. Your initial collaboration may be limited to allowing you to try out a few things within the teacher's existing framework. However, a productive collaborative relationship may eventually lead to co-teaching or even modeling for each other.

To be highly effective in writing collaboration, the library media specialist should be well versed in technologies available to help in the aid of teaching writing. Not only do Web sites and online databases provide students with information, but also other forms of technology can be used to communicate the message to the audience—PowerPoint, video production, publishing software, and emerging technologies that will one day seem as common place as blogs and Wikis. You can provide the big picture by seeing how the project meets standards, trains students to be information literate, and has technology and media resources in mind to help guide the students and teachers through the entire writing process.

Figure 3.1 North Elementary Library Media Center
Collaboration Planning & Teaching Log

Teacher(s): _____
Grade Level: _____ Planning Date: _____ Project Date: _____

Library Information Literacy Standards	Indiana Academic Standards
The student who is information literate • accesses information efficiently & effectively • evaluates information critically & competently • uses information accurately & creatively **The student who is an independent learner is** • information literate & pursues information related to personal interests • information literate & appreciates literature & other creative expressions of information • information literate and strives for excellence in information seeking and knowledge generation **The student who contributes positively to the learning community and to society is** • information literate & recognizes the importance of information to a democratic society • information literate & practices ethical behavior in regard to information & information technology • information literate & participates effectively in groups to pursue & generate information	

Project Description (including estimated timeline & use the back if more room is needed to write):

Teacher will:	Library Media Specialist will:

Resources:	___ Hyperstudio	___ Scanner	Evaluation:
___ Internet	___ WNOR	___	
___ PowerPoint	___ Kid Pix	___	
___ Word	___ Inspiration	___	
___ Excel	___ Digital Cam.	___	

Attach any other handouts, notes, or materials created for the project.

Provide Student Assistance

No matter what the project, the student is going to need information. It may be for a nonfiction report or it might be background information for a time period for a historical fictional tale. You are trained to teach students how to find the information they need. Organizing that information and using it for a completed project is a skill difficult to master. It will require both you and the classroom teacher working together to put students on the right path. Teachers will appreciate your help in knowing how to organize those lessons with students and perhaps sharing the role of instruction. You can provide technological skills to help students create a variety of final products based on the writing and research. This knowledge allows students to expand beyond the confines of the classroom and at the same time builds trust between you and teachers—a win win for all.

In this age of information, it is important that we continue to work with students to follow ethical use of information. No matter what type of writing they may be doing, it is critical that they cite their sources. Avoiding plagiarism and setting up healthy habits early will serve students well in the future. While you should not be the copyright police, library media specialists should be well versed in the laws and be able to offer instruction to students in avoiding plagiarism and on the ethical use of information. Teachers and students will rely on you to help guide them down the straight and narrow—whether they really want to go that way or not.

Provide Resources

The library media center creates a centralized location of resources that can be shared throughout the building. Using the library media center as a clearinghouse for resources can help students and teachers. In writing, it is helpful for students to see sample work that has been assessed—commonly referred to as anchor papers. These anchor papers help students to see what they need to do to obtain a successful score on a writing project. The library media center can be a warehouse for some of these resources where students can easily view others' work. Obviously it is critical that the line is drawn as to viewing someone's work and plagiarizing it. It may be that the library media center maintains these materials in the professional collection for faculty to access at the point of need. Whatever system is in place, it is important that students have anchor papers to help them determine where the bar is they need to reach. See the Works Consulted section at the end of the chapter for anchor paper sources.

Library media centers have long been a resource for the traditional research paper. Electronic resources have expanded an individual school's ability to offer quality and quantity of resources for students and teachers. Both primary and secondary resources are important for students to have available as they begin to research and finally to write their end product. You can help them to learn how to use these resources effectively. By having conversations with teachers, you will have the appropriate resources when needed. By planning in advance, time is available for ordering and processing new materials or to seek out funding for additional resources.

Library media specialists should constantly be looking at the big picture and how the resources in the library media center can support school wide initiatives. Take time to add subject headings to books that are good examples of beginnings and endings. It will help both students and teachers in finding resources to use as models when writing. Use the library's Web page to highlight online resources such as dictionaries, clip-art for picture files, and an online thesaurus.

Taking time to focus on the needs of all those involved will allow a stronger bond to form during the collaborative process. In turn, that too should create a better learning opportunity for students.

One More Thing...

It is important to take time to plan instruction with teachers. It may prove helpful to plan out how you are going to start collaborating with teachers. Find the teacher you think will be the most receptive and start with him or her. Start simple, too. Collaborative endeavors do not have to be full-scale projects. It could be a simple focus lesson that you provide on how to access databases, or how to come up with adjectives to make writing more interesting.

Works Consulted

Bishop, Kay. *Connecting Libraries with Classrooms: the Curricular Roles of the Media Specialist.* Worthington, OH: Linworth, 2003.

Buzzeo, Toni. *Collaborating to Meet Standards: Teacher/Librarian Partnerships for 7-12.* Worthington, OH: Linworth, 2002.

Buzzeo, Toni. *Collaborating to Meet Standards: Teacher/Librarian Partnerships for K-6.* Worthington, OH: Linworth, 2002.

Holcomb, Edie L. *Asking the Right Questions: Techniques for Collaboration and School Change.* Thousands Oak, CA: Corwin Press, 2001.

Johnson, Doug. *Learning Right from Wrong in the Digital Age: An Ethics Guide for Parents, Teachers, Librarians, and Others Who Care about Computer-Using Young People.* Worthington, OH: Linworth, 2003.

Simpson, Carol. *Copyright for Schools: A Practical Guide. 4th ed.* Worthington, OH: Linworth, 2005.

Tamm, James W., and Robert J. Luyet. *Radical Collaboration.* New York: Harper Business, 2004.

Chapter 4

Prewrite

> *Prewrite is any event that leads to a final product of writing.*
> *Confucius said "A journey of a thousand miles begins with a single step." Think*
> *of prewriting as the step that gets writing started. In the previous chapters, you*
> *were introduced to prewrite as the beginning of the writing process. During*
> *this stage, writers define the topic, audience, purpose, focus, overall message,*
> *organization, and voice. If students are conducting research, they consider the*
> *most appropriate research model.*

Provide Teacher Assistance

Student Choice of Topic

Although writers should choose their topics so they can bring meaning to subjects, any day in the typical school makes it clear that teachers often give writing assignments. These range from assigned topics for journal writing to a report about a specific state or a biography about a scientist. The prevalence of assigned topics reflects a lack of understanding of the writing process as well as how topics might appropriately be assigned or when students should choose the topic. While assigned topics can develop content knowledge in a given discipline, foster higher-level thinking, and assess student understanding, they inhibit intrinsic motivation for writing. Students need sustained experiences in writing about their lives and thoughts to see writing as communication. When students learn how to choose their own topics and experience the pleasure that comes from an audience showing interest in their everyday lives, thoughts, successes, and struggles, they want to write and revise.

    In your conversations with teachers, you will likely hear that assigned topics are usually connected to high-stakes assessment. Writing samples are included in many standardized tests. In some states, writing standards carry equal weight with reading standards. Those standards are often tested through prompted writing samples, so students do need some experience in that format. However, prompted writing should not be the mainstay of the writing program.

> *Discuss with teachers the advantages and disadvantages of giving students writing prompts and when student choice is important or essential. Using this guideline, students should choose their topic when motivation for writing is a problem, when students are learning a new mode of writing such as persuasion, and when students have not seen the value in revision. Assigned topics are best when teachers are administering quarterly writing assessments or when knowledge of a topic is being developed or assessed.*

Even when assigned topics are appropriate, the teacher can let students narrow the assigned topic to a personalized level by writing from their point of view or selecting what aspect of the topic they want to address. For example, when assigned to write about the Middle Ages, some students will choose to explain the feudal system while others will share knowledge of the mode of dress and the fashions during that time. Giving students choices during prewriting enhances motivation. Knowing the importance of student choice of topics may give you opportunities to discuss with teachers the importance of student choice of topics and to reflect on changes that should be made.

Prewriting Organization

Discuss with teachers ways to promote student choice of topics by having a list of topics and artifacts from students' lives in the system they currently use for writing. Many students keep writing folders and use them throughout the school year to keep their writing in order. Others keep their writing on a computer in their personal file.

> *One way to be sure that students get to write about topics of their interests is to let them start a topics booklet. Begin with an 8½ x 11 paper. Fold the paper in fourths. Label each quarter with a topic such as people, food, places, and hobbies. Let the students add ideas that they know about or would like to know about under each topic. The paper stays in the folder and students chose topics from it throughout the year.*

Another way for writers to keep thoughts flowing for writing is to maintain a writing folder/box that they can continually add items to as they find them. It could include photos, newspaper articles, or music. Figure 4.2 on page 60 provides a sample collaborative lesson for another way to accomplish the task of topic gathering.

When we work with students, we begin by sharing our writing notebooks with them. In each case, while the container is different, there are lists, notes, photographs, and tidbits from our lives. Susan has a voided check for $1,081.00 that she accidentally wrote for a $47.36 bill. She keeps this in her writing folder as a reminder of the time that instead of writing the amount of the bill she wrote the check number for the amount. This check helps her think about all of the times that she has been in too much of a hurry and what happened as a result. Perhaps before you begin sharing the importance of student choice of topics with teachers, you will want to organize your own writing notebook as an example.

Provide Student Assistance

Prewrite Possibilities

Students utilize their own experiences as background for their writing. Thus, any event that leads to writing becomes a "prewrite." As a library media specialist, you can go beyond the typical prewrite experiences of the classroom. Consider the following possibilities.

- Provide all kinds of reading material for prewriting inspiration. If writers are trying to generate an inquiry question for a research project, reading widely can help students generate the topic and the focus of the research. Responding to literature helps readers become more aware of the books, newspapers, magazines, or graphic novels that they read. Students, who know they will be writing about what they read, read more carefully.

- Allow students to share their ideas in meaningful ways instead of the traditional book report formats. Assemble a combination of notes, sketches, photographs, quick-writes, graphic organizers, and lists. Show how they could be used to tell about books. The variety of options encourages them to write about their reading.

- Signal students that a planned experience will serve as a part of their prewrite. Physical or virtual fieldtrips provide exciting learning opportunities for students, but writing about them gives further meaning to students. For example, zoo trips take place at several grade levels. Children often write animal reports before or after the experience. Social studies units include a study of community helpers and can include trips to the police station, firehouse, and hospital. Thank you letters often follow the trips.

- Intermediate and middle school students get to attend plays or community musical performances. They often have to write a reflection of the event.

- High school students get involved in local community affairs and relay the experience to their social study classes. Their jobs, extra-curricular activities, and hobbies also provide a basis for writing.

- Promote music from various time periods to help students gain a new perspective of the era. Social studies comes alive through experiencing the music and movies of the time studied. Some schools play music as students enter the building. Writing about the music or songwriters personalizes the experiences for listeners.

- Incorporate art. Art teachers open the eyes of their students to a plethora of possibilities through paintings, sculpture, and the people who create them. The Internet makes it possible to view art pieces from around the world. As students view the paintings or sculpture, they gain new understanding. Art can act as a catalyst for sharing opinions and understanding about the topic of their writing.

- Capture the excitement of sporting events as sports fans use their writing skills in a variety of ways. Students write about their favorite sports star or create a "newspaper article" about their own team's latest match or game. In physical education class, they write out the rules to make it clear that they know the teacher's expectations.

Think about the Audience

After writers decide their topics, they must always keep in mind who will read the writing. You can assist students in keeping focused on their audience by asking writers the following questions.

- Does the audience have minimal background knowledge of the subject or are they experts?
- Will they want to know details or are they interested only in the "big picture?"
- Would graphics add understanding to the topic for this audience or will they respond better to text alone?
- What does the writer think the audience will find most interesting about the topic?

Know the Purpose

As writers work their way through the prewrite activities, they need to think about the purpose of their writing. Library media specialists often help students discern the purpose as they talk about the audience and topic. Carl usually asks students, "What do you most want your readers to know, understand, believe, or be able to do as a result of your writing?"

Get Focused

As students work on their writing, they must ask questions to help themselves stay focused. This makes a great time for the library media specialist to introduce graphic organizers, either in a paper format or with software such as Inspiration/Kidspiration or Cmap Tools.

- What is the purpose of my writing?
- Who is the audience for my writing?
- What do I know about the topic?
- What about the topic interests me?
- Do I need to research?
- What type of product will I create?

As students explore their options and ask questions, they are ready to narrow the topic. You can help students move from the broad topic of "dogs" to a personalized interest of "what kind of dog would be suitable for a family with children?"

Library media specialists can also assist students in this part of the process by making them aware of the resources available on the topic. For example, Carl struggled to help a student find information about a "football fish." After the two looked in several places but found very little, the student decided on a different topic with more available resources. After narrowing the topic, writers may need to re-ask some of the questions above to be sure they continue to move in the right direction.

Use Research Processes

Students often need to know more about their topic. Research can provide additional information. There are numerous research processes, some of which are listed in alphabetical order (see Figure 4.1 on page 54). If a school district has chosen a process and uses it throughout the grades and district, students get accustomed to it and use it more effectively than if each teacher starts his own system. You can help get that process in place and provide consistency for students.

Deliver a Message

With a topic, audience, purpose, and research model chosen, writers start to think about their message. The message answers the question, "What is the one thing you want the reader to know about your topic?" In classrooms where Susan worked recently, the students had been assigned to write descriptions of a special place in their house. Many had picked their bedrooms and the writing all sounded the same. A review of the prewrite webs showed the problem. At the center of the web, students had "my room." In her focus lesson Susan modeled how to consider the message about their special place. She modeled by changing "my bedroom" to "my room—family gathering place." As she constructed her web and wrote from it, the students could see that the details one includes are connected to the message. Susan's writing did not sound like a blueprint of her bedroom, instead it reflected the sharing of stories, discussions about friends, problem solving, and silliness that grew out of raising her girls. The students in the classroom constructed new webs with their message in the center.

One important caution about forming the message during prewriting: stay flexible. Since writing is discovery, the message may change during drafting and revision. As the writer works, it becomes evident sometimes, even frequently, that the point, message, or plot is taking a different turn. Writers should have the freedom to change their message and perspective as they continue to write and revise.

Plan Organization

As students continue through prewriting, they need to start organizing the information. Organization is especially important if research is a part of prewrite. Taking notes allows writers to capture some of the ideas they read. They may choose to use pencil and paper or a computer. Either way, students need to be taught how to paraphrase the ideas they encounter in the writing of others.

Figure 4.1   Research Processes — Samples

Research Name and Contact Information	Creators	Overview
The Big6 <www.big6.com>	Mike Eisenberg and Bob Berkowitz	1. Task Definition 2. Information Seeking Strategies 3. Location and Access 4. Use of Information 5. Synthesis 6. Evaluation
Information Search Process <scils.rutgers.edu/~kuhlthau/News/ISPchapter.htm>	Carol Kuhlthau	1. Initiation 2. Selection 3. Exploration 4. Formulation 5. Collection 6. Presentation
Kids Connect Toolbox <www.ala.org/ala/aasl/schlibrariesandyou/k12students/aaslkctools.htm>	American Library Association	1. I wonder… 2. I find… 3. I evaluate… 4. I share…
Savvy Seven <www.lmcsource.com/consultants/savvy7.html>	Nancy Miller and Connie Champlin	1. What is the Question? 2. What Resources Should I Use? 3. How Do I Find the Information? 4. How Do I Gather the Information? 5. Which Information Do I Use? 6. How Do I Share What I Learned? 7. How Do I Evaluate My Work?

Figure 4.1   Research Processes — Samples

Research Name and Contact Information	Creators	Overview
William and Mary Research Model \<cfge.wm.edu/ TeachingModels/ ResearchModel.htm\>	Center for Gifted Education, The College of William & Mary, Williamsburg, VA	1. Identify your issue or problem. 2. Read about your issue and identify points of view or arguments through information sources. 3. Form a set of questions that can be answered by a specific set of data. 4. Gather evidence through research techniques such as surveys, interviews, or analysis of primary and secondary source documents. 5. Manipulate and transform data so that it can be interpreted. 6. Draw conclusions and make inferences. 7. Determine implications and consequences. 8. Communicate your findings. (Prepare an oral presentation for classmates based on note cards and written report.)
8 Ws of Information Inquiry \<eduscapes.com/info/ topic71.htm\>	Annette Lamb	1. Watching (Exploring) 2. Wondering (Questioning) 3. Webbing (Searching) 4. Wiggling (Evaluating) 5. Weaving (Synthesizing) 6. Wrapping (Creating) 7. Waving (Communicating) 8. Wishing (Assessing)

Graphic organizers, such as the following list, can also assist children in keeping their information in order.

- KWL Chart – What I Know - What I Want to Know - What I Learned
- Quick Bib Form – Author, Title, Publishing Company or Site, Copyright Date
- Research Triangle – Larger idea is at the top of the wide side of the triangle, questions are asked to narrow the topic, and the final question is at the narrow end of the triangle.

Use Primary and Secondary Sources

As students look at sources, you can help them understand the difference between primary and secondary sources. Primary sources come from original records created during the time period being studied or by someone who participated in the event. Secondary sources reflect ideas of someone who did not participate in the actual event, but are based on primary sources. Primary sources give a sense of immediacy to the topic, while secondary sources often give a more long-term perspective to it. Using a search engine and the phrases "primary sources" and "secondary sources" will reveal current Web listings. Careful observation of print materials shows whether they depict primary or secondary sources.

When reading the sources, students need to have a sense of which ones give appropriate information and which might be less helpful. For example:

- Does the author have experiences or education that makes her an expert on the topic?
- Does the author or represented organization have an inherent bias on the topic?
- What is the copyright date? What influential events concerning the topic have occurred since that time?

As students gather information from a wide range of sources, their topic emphasis may change. They need to continue to reframe their specific questions as they read about the topic. Sometimes after reading a wide range of materials, students get distracted with all the information and need assistance with focusing on a narrow topic. You can help students concentrate on a reasonable topic choice by reminding them of the audience and purpose of the writing project.

Compile Sources

Keeping the sources cited and information up-to-date while researching means that facet of the writing is complete at the end of the writing project. Library media specialists can help articulate that expectation across the grade levels. Even young children need to know the author and title of the materials they use. As they progress through elementary school, they should add copyright date, publishing company, and location information. They may use a fill-in chart to track their citing sources information. Middle school students need to follow a prescribed bibliographic format. High school English departments often have made a decision about the writing style they think is most appropriate for their students. You can adapt that style to work for younger students, too.

Color coding the sources can help to keep information organized. For example, put the titles in red, authors in blue, and the publishing company information in green. A key depicts the plan.

Many teachers create ground rules for writing that you need to know so you can remind students of the rules as they work in the library media center. Ground rules may be as simple as "Write in complete sentences." If there are school-wide rules, posting them on a bulletin board makes sense. If the rules vary by teacher, keeping a folder in the library media center of the rules by teachers' names allows students to easily access them. When working with students, you need to have a clear understanding of teachers' expectations.

Children also write from their own needs, instead of a teacher-made assignment. Youngsters' experiences on a sports team provide real-life experiences that make great entries in a journal. Sharing the thrill of a piano or dance recital make great topics to share in a letter or e-mail to friends or family. Children use writing to chronicle their emotions and moods as well as their relationships with others. The writing may appear as short stories or poetry. Library media specialists encourage personal writing by introducing literature that includes that type of writing to students, sharing their own writing, including students' writing in the library media center collection, or creating a local student writers' group.

Stay Focused

Students sometimes get so excited over their topics that they have trouble keeping focused on their writing purpose as they read and research. You can help writers stay focused on tasks in several ways. Refer students back to their graphic organizers. Keep teachers' assignments in a folder or post them on bulletin boards in the library media center so that students can access them. Explore with students what most appealed to them about the topic because their enthusiasm should show through in their writing.

Tell students how published writers learn more about their topic than they actually put into their books. Most videos or CDs about authors and illustrators speak to how they go through the creative process, which makes a great connection for students when they hear their favorite author's and illustrator's view on the process and how difficult they find it to keep focused.

Point out to students the authors' purpose as books appear in classroom and library media center instruction. Connect to curriculum. All schools teach math. They do it in a variety of ways. Regardless of the math methodology, trade books can be included in students' experiences. A picture book, Pigs at Odds focuses on probability and can be used with any age learning that math concept. The author intended for readers to enjoy a story and practice probability. As you point out the authors' purpose in read-aloud literature, students start to look for it in their own reading and then apply the idea in their writing.

English classrooms often read classic literature. The Eyewitness Classics series includes stories, background facts, and photographs. The authors focus on the original story, as well as give a perspective to current literature. They want readers to get the flavor of the original text and understand it more clearly than if they just read it in its entirety.

In social studies and science, students learn about people of importance. Biographers want their readers to know about the books' subjects. When students read two biographies about the same person from different authors, they start to see how the authors treat the same incidents differently. That can start a discussion about the authors' purposes and how they are reflected in their writing. Students learn to think about the authors' purpose as they read all kinds of books.

Decide the Voice

Writers personalize their communication when writing in print as obviously as when they talk to one another. As students write, their personalities should shine through their word choices. Including personal details about the topic makes it come alive. Emotions can permeate the page through punctuation! Where appropriate, a sense of humor can add enjoyment to writing for the author and the audience. Voice provides a clear point of view or perspective about the topic.

Library media specialists help students better understand voice when they expose writers to a variety of voices in literature. Reading aloud books that portray different voices and talking about that characteristic with children gives them background knowledge to the topic. Students will start to be aware of the voice of some of their favorite authors, once you and the classroom teacher talk about the concept. Jon Scieszka writes in a humorous voice in *Math Curse*, a picture book that entertains all ages. Andrew Clements enchants readers with a more serious tone in chapter book stories of students, such as *The Landry News*. High schoolers get a new view of poetry's voice through Mel Glenn's work like *Jump Ball: A Basketball Season in Poems*. Start with books from the Prewrite Literature Connections at the end of the chapter and then add your own personal favorites to the list.

One More Thing...

Prewriting provides the first step in the writing journey. During this part of the process, writers define the topic, audience, purpose, focus, overall message, organization, and voice. They consider research processes. Effective prewriting lays the foundation for success throughout the writing process.

Inexperienced writers tend to miss the importance of prewriting and rush into drafting. Your awareness of the power of prewriting for focus and voice will be useful in conversations with students and their teachers.

Literature Connections

Axelrod, Amy. *Pigs at Odds: Fun with Math and Games*. New York: Simon & Schuster, 2000.

Brown, Marc. *Arthur Writes a Story*. New York: Little, Brown, 1996.

Cleary, Beverly. *Dear Mr. Henshaw*. New York: Avon Books, 1996.

Clements, Andrew. *The Landry News*. New York: Simon & Schuster Children's, 1999.

Falconer, Ian and Edith. *Olivia Journal*. New York: Andrews McMeel Publishing, 2003.

Glenn, Mel. Jump Ball: *A Basketball Season in Poems*. New York: Penguin Young Readers Group, 1997.

Krulik, Nancy. *Write On!* New York: Penguin Putnam Books for Young Readers, 2005.

Little, Jean. *Hey World, Here I Am!* New York: HarperCollins Children's Books, 1991.

Nixon, Joan Lowery. *If You Were a Writer*. New York: Simon & Schuster Children's, 1995.

Park, Barbara. *Top-Secret Personal Beeswax*. New York: Random House Books for Young Readers, 2003.

Rylant, Cynthia. *Mr. Putter and Tabby Write the Book*. New York: Harcourt Children's Books, 2005.

Schotter, Roni. *Nothing Ever Happens on 90th Street*. New York: Scholastic, Inc., 1999.

Scieszka, Jon. *Math Curse*. New York: Viking Juvenile, 1995.

Snicket, Lemony. *The Blank Book (A Series of Unfortunate Events)*. New York: HarperCollins Children's Books, 2004.

Series

Dear America. New York: Scholastic, Inc.

Eyewitness Classics. New York: Dorling Kindersley.

Works Consulted

Barry in a Box: Video Lessons in Revision with Barry Lane for Grades 3-8. Barry Lane. Marianne Mosely. Videocassette. Discover Writing Videos, 2002.

CmapTools. IHMC – A University Affiliated Research Institute. 4 Jun. 2006. <cmap.ihmc.us>.

Inspiration/Kidspiration Software. Inspiration Software Inc. 4 Jun. 2006. <www.inspiration.com/home.cfm>.

Figure 4.2 Research Process Samples
Library Media Center Collaboration Planning & Teaching Log

Teacher(s): _____
Grade Level: K-1 _____ Planning Date: _____ Project Date: _____

Information Literacy Standards Standards 1, 2, and 3 NETS Standards Standard 5	Academic Standards English/Language Arts Essential Question What topics interest me? What might I like to write about?

Idea Web

Project Description:
20 minutes

Students will create a web that reflects topics of interest to them.

Sample Student Product

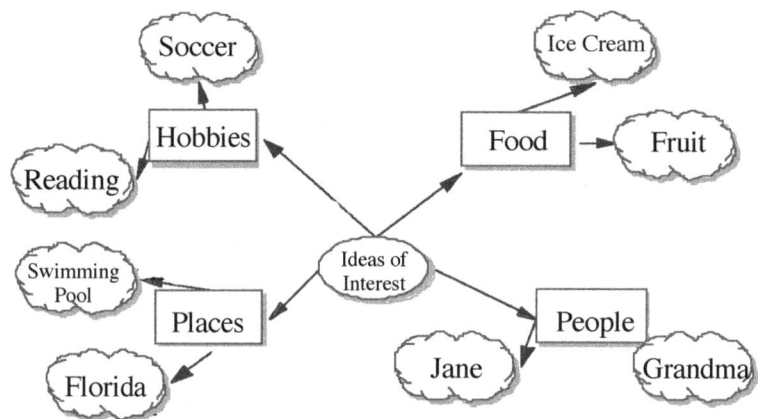

Teacher will: Direct students to use the teacher-created Kidspiration/Inspiration web file and add at least two ideas for each topic. They should be ideas that interest the individual students. They may add additional ideas during the year. Words or pictures may represent the ideas.	Library Media Specialist will: Model creating a mind map. Assist students with any technical questions concerning the software.
Resources: Inspiration/Kidspiration software, Word processing software, or paper and pencil.	Student Assessment: Students will check to be sure they have added at least two ideas to the mind map. Teacher and LMS will use a rubric that reflects software use as well as ideas. Project Evaluation: Teacher/LMS periodically checks mind maps throughout the year.

Attach any other handouts, notes, or materials created for the project.

Figure 4.3 Sources Cited
Library Media Center Collaboration Planning & Teaching Log

Teacher(s): _____
Grade Level: 2-5 _____ Planning Date: _____ Project Date: _____

Information Literacy Standards Standard 3	Academic Standards English/Language Arts
NETS Standards Standard 5	Essential Question Have I given credit to the sources that I used?

Sources Cited

Project Description:
1 hour

Students will give credit to the sources they use in their research.

Sample Student Product

Author Last Name, Author First Name. <u>Title</u>. *Company Location:* Publishing Company, Date.

Brown, Marc. <u>Arthur Writes a Story</u>. *New York:* Little, Brown, & Company, 1998.

Teacher will: Display the sources cited model in the classroom. Set expectations in assignments that sources will be cited.	Library Media Specialist will: Create an age-appropriate model of sources cited and display it in the LMC and on the school Web site. Teach how to do a works cited sheet.
Resources: Word processing software or paper and pencil.	Student Assessment: Students will check their works cited list against models. Teacher and LMS will check students' works cited list as assignments are submitted. Project Evaluation: Teacher and LMS will discuss other optional sources and ways to display the model.

Attach any other handouts, notes, or materials created for the project.

Prewrite

Figure 4.4 Note-Taking
Library Media Center Collaboration Planning & Teaching Log

Teacher(s): _____
Grade Level: 6-8 _____ Planning Date: _____ Project Date: _____

Information Literacy Standards Standards 1, 2, and 3 NETS Standards Standard 5	Academic Standards English/Language Arts Essential Question Which of the pieces of information I read will help me develop my topic?

Note-Taking

Project Description:
Two hours

Students will capture important ideas from their reading that they may use in their writing.

Sample Student Product

Source	Animal	Preferred Food	Animal's Size	Is this animal often a pet?
Smith, John. Man's Best Friend. New York: Good Books, 2003. Pages 10 and 11	Dog	Dog food	3 lbs. to 50 lbs.	yes
Jones, June. Cats for You and Me. New York: Pet Books, 2004. Pages 4 and 5	Cat	Cat food	3 lbs. to 15 lbs.	yes

Teacher will: Work with the LMS to create a matrix. Assist students with topic selection Direct students to read at least five sources and fill in their matrix. Remind them that they do not have to use complete sentences.	**Library Media Specialist will:** Work with the teacher to create a matrix. Assist students with topic selection. Model using the matrix.
Resources: Assorted sources, word processing software or paper and pencil	**Student Assessment:** Students will highlight the two sources they found most helpful. Teacher and LMS will check students' matrixes. **Project Evaluation:** Teachers/LMS will check that five sources were used and note the validity of the two that students chose as most helpful.

Attach any other handouts, notes, or materials created for the project.

Figure 4.5 LP Accepting-Rejecting Sources
Library Media Center Collaboration Planning & Teaching Log

Teacher(s): _____
Grade Level: 9-12 _____ Planning Date: _____ Project Date: _____

Information Literacy Standards Standard 2	Academic Standards English/Language Arts
NETS Standards Standard 5	Essential Question Which sources give the most accurate information on my topic?

Accepting/Rejecting Sources

Project Description:
Three hours

Students look at four sample sources and fill in the following questionnaire to evaluate the sources.

Sample Student Work

Source Information - Author Last Name, Author First Name. <u>Title</u>. Company Location: Publishing Company, Date. or Web site Name. Date Accessed. Web Address.
1. Does the author or Web site have authority in the field?
2. Does the author or Web site have an inherent bias, because of relationship to a company or organization?
3. Is there contact information for the author/site?
4. What is the copyright date or site updating date?
5. Did you find the information in another source?

Teacher will: Introduce three sources to students. Assist students as they work on the assignment.	Library Media Specialist will: Introduce three sources to students. Model evaluating a source. Assist students as they work on the assignment.
Resources: Word processing software or paper and pencil	Student Assessment: Students will mark their two best sources on a chart of the sources. Teacher and LMS will check off the students' chart. Project Evaluation: Teacher and LMS check students' charts and discuss the students' responses.

Attach any other handouts, notes, or materials created for the project.

Prewrite

Chapter 5

Drafting

> *Drafting occurs when writers put their ideas onto paper or into a computer.*
>
> *Since drafting is communication with an audience, writers need to concentrate on getting their ideas down instead of the mechanics of writing. Focus on spelling, capitalization, and grammar comes later during editing. Students will create one or more drafts, depending on the amount they revise. As we have already discussed, students often want to have their first draft be the final draft. This chapter will provide ideas to help library media specialists move students out of that mindset.*

Provide Teacher Assistance

Encourage Drafts

When writers begin drafting, the teacher can be instrumental in helping writers sustain their effort and enthusiasm for the piece they are drafting. Suggest checking drafts and making positive comments as an ongoing part of the writer's workshop block. Writers may also need to pause during the drafting stage to share with a peer and receive affirmation that the piece is worth continuing.

Provide Student Assistance

Model Drafting

By the time writers begin drafting, they have usually determined their purpose, audience, topic, and possibly message. If students "do not know what to say," discuss with them what happened in prewriting and ask to see what has been accomplished. Following a successful prewrite, encourage students to write in a free flow method. Model continuous writing as you work with students in the library media center.

Show them what you have done in preparation for drafting. Use whatever you have available: a computer and projector, an overhead, or chart paper. Show them your list from brainstorming, web, sketches, whatever you have used to prepare for drafting. Walk them through your thoughts as you made the transition from prewriting to drafting.

- Which of my ideas are interesting?
- Which ones should I research to get additional information?
- Is there an obvious beginning, middle, and end to the topic?
- What mode of writing would be most appropriate for the topic?
- Where or about what will my audience have the most questions?

With few exceptions, the students you are working with already have experience with drafting. Engage them in sharing how they get their ideas out of their heads onto paper or a computer screen. Emphasize that good writing goes through a series of steps—writing, revising, writing, revising—until the writer is confident that the piece has accomplished his goals. Show students how you accomplish these "multiple drafts" on the same piece, without recopying or starting over. Your modeling will make it clear that good writing is not done 15 minutes before an assignment is due nor does it require starting from scratch each time.

> *Library media specialists often see students as they prewrite and draft. Encourage students to come back and share their drafts in the library media center. Keep a writing display area on a wall, in notebooks, or on the library media center Web page or blog to share works in process. Keep writing tools such as paper, pencils, computer disks/drives in the library media center. In a perfect world, students would always carry their own supplies; but in the real world, they sometimes need assistance.*

During the drafting stage, writers may become stuck, not knowing what to say next. Provide them with the assurance that a block is often a sign that the writer needs to pause and do some of the same kinds of thinking that occurred during prewrite. Put them in touch with the wisdom of published authors to show options for solving the problems they face. Share the tips and experiences from prolific authors by viewing videos and providing students with quotes.

For example, in *Anonymously Yours*, Richard Peck shares insight into his writing. In *My Own Two Feet*, prolific author Beverly Cleary tells about her experience in creating her first published book, *Henry Huggins*.

Research for writing can take many forms. In *How I Came to Be a Writer*, Phyllis Reynolds Naylor tells about some of the phone calls she has made to get more information for her writing.

She has called places such as the following:

- The Civil Aeronautics Board to find out to what altitude a plane rises when taking off from Santa Fe.
- A dentist to find out how long dental records are kept.
- A lawyer to find out the steps in prosecuting someone for income tax evasion.
- A family service agency to ask how they handle cases of child abuse.
- An ophthalmologist to ask about the treatment of crossed eyes.
- An undertaker to find out how long a wooden casket would last six feet under. (68)

Students sometimes have difficulty creating names for their characters. They start to understand that even professionally published authors work diligently at the task when they read Sid Fleischman's comments about names in *The Abracadabra Kid: A Writer's Life*.

In addition, I started the practice of jotting down interesting names as I stumbled across them. I spend a lot of time with my characters trying on and discarding monikers. To a fiction writer a rose by any other name does not smell as sweet. Names resonate. The look and sound of a name often helps me create and fix the character (158).

Discover and Maintain Focus

Drafting can be difficult if students do not know what point they are trying to make. In *The Craft of Revision,* Donald Murray advises writers to "Say One Thing" (62-66). Asking student writers, "What is the one thing that you want your readers to know, understand, believe, or do as a result of your writing?" will often help them discover or maintain their focus. While secondary students have been taught about the importance of a thesis statement, it may be a problem. Beginning with a thesis statement often prevents writers from discovering what they know or believe and restricts them in exploring their thinking. Suggest to them that like the introduction, the thesis statement can be written after the first draft is finished.

Show writers several pieces on the same topic that have different messages or make different points. When Susan works with elementary and secondary students alike, she reminds students of the importance of the message by reading three excerpts from articles about a topic of interest to them. Sometimes she uses articles about the opening of baseball season. Other times Susan chooses letters to the editor written about extending the school day. Begin your own collection of "same topic, different message" writing samples and share them with teachers and students. As students listen to or review each piece, they become more aware of writing styles and the importance of deciding on what type of message the writer wants to deliver.

In narrative writing, the message becomes the plot. Change "What is the one thing that you want your readers to know, understand, believe, or do as a result of your writing?" to "What is it that your characters learn, discover, or accomplish by the end of your story?" Writers of stories can easily get lost in the action during drafting and forget that they are taking their characters on a journey across time, to some end result. During drafting, the writers will develop their characters much as parents see their own children's personalities emerge through daily events.

Share comments of published writers about how they discovered something about their characters during the writing. In *Best Wishes* by Cynthia Rylant, she comments that what she writes often surprises her. Asking students to talk about their characters as if they are real people who they are getting to know often helps them stay connected with their writing. When Susan's oldest daughter was drafting a story about an elf, Susan asked, "Who does he hang around with?" Her daughter replied without hesitation, "I do not know. He has not told me yet."

Use Anchor Papers

> *Anchor papers are samples of student writing that display the qualities and characteristics that teachers expect students to achieve through their teaching. Anchor papers provide models for students to view as they write.*

Seeing skillfully done samples allows writers to get a clear picture of good writing. Showing drafts that correspond to the mode students are using and that have gone through several revisions will be helpful. As students compare and contrast different modes of writing, they use that experience to influence their own work.

In the library media center, display anchor papers of writing as it progressed through the stages. Be sure to include representations of various modes. Keep a notebook of anchor papers in the writing center or on the reference shelf. Look in the Works Consulted section for Web sites featuring anchor papers. Build your own local set of examples by asking students each year to donate their writing to your collection.

Organize Writing

When Marge was a child, she was in a class where they were assigned different people to research. The reports all sounded like a poorly done encyclopedia listing, e.g. she was born…, died…, and was famous for …. They did not know any other way to organize their writing. Knowing about and using different organizational structures would have made for more interesting reports. When students are writing informative pieces, share several treatments of the same topic by displaying articles in magazines and trade books. Guide students so they can see that a given article was organized around a compare and contrast structure or another piece began like a first-hand account but then transitioned into an informative piece with a main idea and supporting details format.

As library media specialists, we know an assortment of informational and recreational materials, and we can introduce our students to them. Professionally published materials use diverse ways to organize information or story lines. Talk with your students about different organizational formats. Even as students read material, they might not think through the structures used, unless you point them out. When your students write animal reports, use a projected view of the sample books to let them see how the similar information might be displayed differently on the page. If they are writing biographies, read aloud the opening page of two different books about the same person. Give them examples of a good first line/paragraph/page and how it draws the reader to delve deeper into the writing. Share some fiction that begins with a flashback. Students might then try starting a short story with a flashback and organizing the plot around more current events.

Figure 5.1 shows some titles to use as samples when teaching students about organizational structures.

After writers get their first draft organized, they need to ask themselves questions similar to the ones modeled by the library media specialist in the draft model lesson:

- How do we know these ideas are accurate or interesting?
- Which ones should we research to get additional information?
- Is there an obvious beginning, middle, and end to the topic?
- How are the main points organized?
- Is there a logical sequence to the writing?

Consider Adding More Information

When Marge was writing a weekly book review column, she would write it and then leave it for 24 hours. She was always surprised at what she found when she returned to it. It always needed more information. At first she wanted to think that gremlins were in her computer and deleting some of the work, but in her more rational moments she knew she just needed to do more drafts. She needed to flesh out the topic.

Student writers will often find that they need to add more information to their work, too. When possible, help teachers create project timelines that allow students to submit drafts as a part of the assessment process. If students are working independently of assigned timelines, talk to them about creating their own timelines that allow for multiple drafts. Just adding more words should not be the goal. The focus should be on creating an improved piece of writing that carries a message effectively from the writer to the reader.

For informational pieces, encourage them to consider the following questions:

- Does the writing fulfill the assignment as the teacher stated it?
- Does the writing give both sides of the issue or make it clear it only represents one side?
- Can someone read the writing without knowing the assignment and make sense of the writing?
- Does the writing leave the reader with questions that should be answered in the writing?

For fiction writing, contemplate the following questions:

- Does the writing fulfill the assignment as the teacher stated it?
- Do the characters' actions make sense for what we know about them?
- Do we know the location, time period, and genre from the details in the story?
- Do we have enough information to "believe" the story?

Figure 5.1 Organizational Structures

Organization Structure	Suggested Literature
Cause and Effect – Events cause specific results	Roberts, Willo Davis. <u>Sugar Isn't Everything</u>. New York: Atheneum, 1997.
Chronological Order – Events appear in the order they happened	Hesse, Karen. <u>Out of the Dust</u>. New York: Scholastic Press, 1997.
Classification Order – A main idea gets broken into smaller segments	Bartoletti, Susan Campbell. <u>Kids on Strike!</u> Boston: Houghton Mifflin, 1999.
Climactic Order – Events appear from the least significant to the most important	Hobbs, Will. <u>Downriver</u>. New York: Macmillan, 1991.
Compare/Contrast Order – Similarities and differences are identified	Simon, Seymour. <u>Animal Fact/Animal Fable</u>. New York: Crown Publishing, 1979.
Flashback/Flash-forward – Flashback (an earlier event appears at the beginning of the story) and flash-forward (a future event appears at the beginning of the story)	Yolen, Jane. <u>The Devil's Arithmetic</u>. New York: Viking, 1988.
Process Order – Events appear in a specific sequence	Lobel, Arnold. <u>On Market Street</u>. New York: Greenwillow, 1981.
Reverse Climactic Order – Events appear from the most important to the least important	Day, Marlis. <u>Why Johnny Died</u>. Pittsburgh: Sterling House, 1999.
Spatial Order – Events move from one location to another	Ryan, Pam Munoz. <u>The Flag We Love</u>. Watertown: Charlesbridge, 1996.

Coordinate Writing Products

Writing takes time. Few writing assignments can be started and completed in one setting. As the library media specialist, you may see the students on an inconsistent basis, but you can assist students with keeping writing products organized.

- Maintain electronic folders on the school server.
- Ask the local pizza shop if pizza boxes could be donated or bought at a discount by the school to store writing projects.
- Keep a computer available to burn CDs so that final work can easily be sent home to parents.
- Buy a supply of thumb drives for the student bookstore or school office to sell, so students can carry their work back and forth from school to home.
- Provide e-mail accounts so students can e-mail their work home and back to school as need be. Of course, your specific school technology policy dictates whether you can use this option.
- As writers work on their drafts, they will likely have to start and stop numerous times. Keep a sign posted in the library media center computer lab that reminds them of how to save their work.

One More Thing…

Drafting can be accomplished in minutes or it may take weeks. We help with this step of the process by encouraging writers to transfer words from their minds to paper or computer and to keep on writing. Student writers often need assurance and concrete evidence that their efforts will result in their ideas being heard, understood, and respected. By showing students examples of early drafts from other writers, including the teachers and library media specialist, linking writer's workshop block to the need for additional prewriting, anticipating their audience's needs and questions, and seeing drafting as a part of the recursive process, students will gain renewed energy to write, explore their own thinking, and communicate with others.

Literature Connections

Bartoletti, Susan Campbell. *Kids on Strike!* Boston: Houghton Mifflin, 1999.

Cleary, Beverly. *My Own Two Feet.* New York: William Morrow, 1995.

Creech, Sharon. *Walk Two Moons.* New York: HarperCollins Children, 1994.

Day, Marlis. *Why Johnny Died.* Pittsburgh: Sterling House, 1999.

Fleischman, Sid. *The Abracadabra Kid: A Writer's Life.* New York: Greenwillow, 1996.

George, Jean Craighead. *Julie of the Wolves.* New York: HarperCollins, 1972.

Hesse, Karen. *Out of the Dust*. New York: Scholastic Press, 1997.

Hobbs, Will. *Downriver*. New York: Macmillan, 1991.

L'Engle, Madeleine. *A Wrinkle in Time*. New York: Farrar, Straus and Giroux, 1962.

Lobel, Arnold. *On Market Street*. New York: Greenwillow, 1981.

Naylor, Phyllis Reynolds. *How I Came to Be a Writer*. New York: Simon & Schuster, 1978.

O'Brien, Robert C. *Mrs. Frisby and the Rats of NIMH*. New York: Simon & Schuster, 1974.

Peck, Richard. *Anonymously Yours*. New York: Simon & Schuster, 1991.

Roberts, Willo Davis. *Sugar Isn't Everything*. New York: Atheneum, 1997.

Ryan, Pam Munoz. *The Flag We Love*. Watertown: Charlesbridge, 1996.

Rylant, Cynthia. *Best Wishes*. New York: Richard C. Owens Publishers, 1992.

Sachar, Louis. *Holes*. New York: Farrar, Straus and Giroux, 1998.

Simon, Seymour. *Animal Fact/Animal Fable*. New York: Crown Publishing, 1979.

Works Consulted

Houghton Mifflin English Grades K-5 Benchmark Papers. 2002. Houghton Mifflin Company. 13 Jun. 2006. <www.eduplace.com/cgi-bin/schtemplate.cgi?template=/rdg/hme/benchmark/index.thtml&grades=k_5&alt=K-5>.

Idaho Direct Writing Assessment Grade 5 (2004-2005) Anchor Papers. 13 Jun. 2006.

<www.sde.state.id.us/instruct/langarts/docs/dwa/grade05/200405Tests/Anchor.htm>.

Murray, Donald M. The Craft of Revision. Rev. 2nd ed. Belmont: Heinle/Thomson Publishers, 2004.

Murray, Donald M. Write to Learn. 8th ed. Belmont: Heinle/Thomson Publishers, 2004.

Murray, Donald M. A Writer Teaches Writing. 5th ed. Boston: Thomson Wadsworth, 2004.

NW Regional Educational Laboratory Assessment - 6+1 Trait Writing. 11 Jan. 2005. Northwest Regional Educational Laboratory. 13 Jun. 2006. <www.nwrel.org/assessment/scoringpractice.php>.

Oregon Department of Education – Scientific Inquiry Anchor Papers. 11 Aug. 2006. Oregon Department of Education. 13 Jun. 2006. <www.ode.state.or.us/search/results/?id=243>

Figure 5.2   Name That Character
Library Media Center Collaboration Planning & Teaching Log

Teacher(s): _____
Grade Level: K-1_____   Planning Date: _____   Project Date:_____

Information Literacy Standards Standard 5	Academic Standards English/Language Arts
NETS Standards Standard 4	Essential Question Which characteristics do I imagine defining my characters?

Name that Character

Project Description:
20 minutes

Students create a list of potential names for their creative writing characters

Sample Student Product Name and characteristics match

Alvin	Small, shy
Betty	Blond, beautiful
Clarissa	Wears a pony tail, loves animals
Don	Brown eyes, likes to play soccer

Teacher will: Model creating characteristics list by starting at the top of the page and writing the alphabet from A to Z. Add names beside each letter of the alphabet. Add characteristics beside each letter of the alphabet.	Library Media Specialist will: Model creating name list by starting at the top of the page and writing the alphabet from A to Z. Add names beside each letter of the alphabet. Add a characteristic to each name.
Resources: LMS needs overhead and transparencies. Students need paper and pencil.	Student Assessment: Students will decide which names and characteristics work best for their creative writing. Teacher and LMS will check alphabet list with names. Project Evaluation: Teacher/LMS note use of various names used in creative writing.

Attach any other handouts, notes, or materials created for the project.

Figure 5.3 If...Then...
Library Media Center Collaboration Planning & Teaching Log

Teacher(s): _____
Grade Level: 2-5 _____ Planning Date: _____ Project Date: _____

Information Literacy Standards Standard 1, 2, 3 NETS Standards Standard 5	Academic Standards English/Language Arts Essential Question What information do I need to know to add details to my writing? Where will I find the information?

If...Then...

Project Description:
30 minutes

Know where to locate information and put it into a T-chart.

Sample Student Product

My Writing

If I Need to Know...	Then Here's Where to Look
When Easter will be in 2010	Calendar
How roads are constructed	Encyclopedia

Teacher will: Create a T-chart with If I Need and Here's Where to Look at the headings. Direct students to read their own writing and find two pieces of information that they need to know to make their writing better. Assist students as they consider information and sources.	Library Media Specialist will: Read aloud Phyllis Reynolds Naylor's *How I Came to Be a Writer,* page 68. Explain how to find information in different places. Give a quick overview of reference tools. Assist students as they consider information and sources.
Resources: Phone books, atlases, encyclopedias, dictionary	**Student Assessment:** Students give pluses on their T-chart to those reference items found most helpful. Teacher and LMS add plus or minus to students' T-charts reflecting time on task and look for additional information in students' writing. Project Evaluation: Teacher and LMS discuss if reference tools met student needs or do additional ones need to be added and how writing was impacted by the additional details.

Attach any other handouts, notes, or materials created for the project.

Figure 5.4 Organization — Flashback/Flash-Forward
Library Media Center Collaboration Planning & Teaching Log

Teacher(s): _____
Grade Level: 6-8 _____ Planning Date: _____ Project Date: _____

Information Literacy Standards Standard 5	Academic Standards English/Language Arts
NETS Standards Standard 4	Essential Question How do I effectively add flashback or flash-forward to my writing?

Organization - Flashback/Flash-Forward

Project Description:
60 minutes

Students see a flashback and flash-forward scenario successfully used in literature.
Create a timeline for their own story and then experiment with flashback or flash-forward.

Sample Student Product – Their story includes either a flashback or flash-forward.

The sunrise made my sleepy five-year-old eyes squint. I wanted to turn over in bed and go back to sleep. Then I remembered…it was my birthday! Birthdays were magical days in our family. I flew out of bed and down the stairs. I bumped my head hard on the dining room door. When I opened my eyes, I looked at my size 13 shoes and wondered if my shoe size would continue to grow. I hoped turning "sweet 16" would bring the joy that being a preschooler had brought.

Teacher will: Tell students to create a timeline of their stories. Add a flashback/flash-forward to the events. Assist students as they work on their writing.	Library Media Specialist will: Define flashback (an earlier event appears at the beginning of the story) and flash-forward (a future event appears at the beginning of the story). She reads aloud specific chapters in the chosen book. Schedule the computer lab or laptop computers. Explain how to use Timeliner software or create a timeline using word processing software.
Resources: Literature featuring Flashback - *Holes* by Louis Sachar (chapter 6/7), *Mrs. Frisby and the Rats of NIMH* by Robert C. O'Brien, *Julie of the Wolves* by Jean Craighead George, *The Devil's Arithmetic* by Jane Yolen, or *Walk Two Moons* by Sharon Creech. Literature featuring Flash-forward - *A Wrinkle in Time* by Madeleine L'Engle.	Student Assessment: Students will fill out a checklist that reflects their experience with the software and writing experience. Teachers and library media specialist will add their observations on the checklist. Project Evaluation: Teachers and library media specialist will discuss the project, consider additional literature and look at the students' checklist responses to the experience.

Attach any other handouts, notes, or materials created for the project.

Drafting

Figure 5.5 Memory Mining
Library Media Center Collaboration Planning & Teaching Log

Teacher(s): _____
Grade Level: 9-12 _____ Planning Date: _____ Project Date: _____

Information Literacy Standards Standard 4	Academic Standards English/Language Arts
NETS Standards Standard 4	Essential Question Which of my childhood memories could I put into writing?

Memory Mining

Project Description:
60 minutes

Retrieve childhood memories that could be used in writing. Create a written snapshot of the memories.

Sample Student Product
When I was a little girl, we used to visit my grandmother on her farm. One night my older brother camped out overnight with me there. That night was one of my favorite events from my childhood, because I loved sleeping in a tent and enjoying a special night with my brother.

This event could be developed into a segment of a coming-of-age story.

Teacher will:	Library Media Specialist will:
Model for students pulling an event from their memory and writing about it. Encourage their memories by mentioning hobbies, family members, holidays, vacations, etc. Ask students to remember something from last week, six months ago, and five or ten years ago. Give students time to write about a specific memory.	Display Beverly Cleary books to remind students of her work. She reads aloud pages 248-252 from *My Own Two Feet,* where Cleary delves into her memory to create her first book. Encourage students as they write personal memories. Talk with students about how it might be used in additional writing.
Resources: *My Own Two Feet* by Beverly Cleary, paper and pencil, or computers with word processing software	**Student Assessment:** Students will write a paragraph that reflects two good aspects and two ways to improve this experience. The paragraph should be at the end of the personal memory writing. Teacher and LMS will create a rubric to assess the final draft of the personal memory writing. **Project Evaluation:** Teacher and LMS will discuss the project and consider additional literature for models.

Attach any other handouts, notes, or materials created for the project.

Chapter 6

Revision

> *Revision is the stage where writers rework their piece to make their ideas and information clearer and more meaningful to the reader.*
>
> *Since revise means to "see again" or to reconsider and alter, writers should reread their draft to consider how to clarify and extend the meaning of the piece for their audience. While revision is a distinct stage in the writing process, some revision has probably already occurred during drafting. Students may have paused to rework a section or to change a word to a more precise one.*

Once writers formally enter the revision stage, they concentrate on making changes that increase the reader's understanding, enjoyment, and interest in the piece by:

- adding information where there are gaps or where confusion is likely.
- reorganizing information by moving it from one place in the piece to another.
- deleting a word, phrase, sentence, or section that strays from the purpose.
- substituting one word, phrase, or example for another.

In Chapter Two you read that revision needs to be a distinct step from editing. When revision is not distinct and done before editing, writers and their teachers may get distracted from improving the quality of the ideas by focusing on spelling and punctuation errors. In the next section, we explore ways that you can work with classroom teachers to make revision the heart of the writing process and make students see value, if not enjoy the step.

Provide Teacher Assistance

Although it is the heart of the writing process, most teachers and writers struggle with revision. Many teachers report that many students enter the revision stage reluctantly. Perhaps, like their adult counterparts, students have worked so hard to get their ideas in print that they simply do not want to change anything. Resistance to revision can be reduced in a number of ways.

- Students will be more receptive to making changes when they are writing about what they know and care about.
- When writers get feedback from their peers, they may realize that without changes, their readers will be confused or lose interest.
- If teachers have consistently modeled revision of their own writing, students will see the benefit of revision and the ease with which it can be done.
- When teachers place students in charge of deciding what needs to be revised, the process goes more smoothly.
- Wise teachers do not overwhelm or discourage their students. They show students how to make a few important changes without recopying.
- Students expect to revise when they have experienced a consistent message from teachers that "Writing is communication."

Two Phases to Revision

In Chapter Two we suggested that revision has two phases that are usually blended. In phase one of revision, the writer decides if the overall message or purpose is clear and if there are any sections that need major attention. Sometimes the conclusion is weak or a section in the middle of the piece sounds awkward. In the second phase, the writer has solved major problems and concentrates on polishing the writing by reworking it a sentence or section at a time.

Discuss with teachers whether they are planning on a "one pass" revision to solve one or two major problems, or if they are planning on polishing the writing by working though one section or trait at a time. Being aware that not every part of the writing needs to be revised is helpful in terms of management.

Provide Student Assistance

Model Setting Priorities for Revision

Share your writing with students. Show them how you returned to your first draft to make simple changes that improved the piece. Explain that revision usually begins with simple questions that writers can ask themselves or their intended audience as they listen to the first draft.

- Is my message or purpose clear?
- Are there gaps in the piece that will create questions or lead to confusion for the reader?
- Are there any sections that I know just are not working?
- Have I included unnecessary information that is not relevant to my purpose?

Sometimes when modeling, you may want to share your first draft and the final draft. Let students listen to the first draft and offer positive comments, questions, or suggestions. Show them the final draft and note how many of their first draft concerns you addressed in your revision. Ask students for their thoughts on how your revisions improved their understanding or enjoyment.

Other times, you can work from the first draft, thinking aloud about what is working and not working. Show students how you can use one or more of the revision tools to make changes without recopying. Demonstrate how you use arrows to move things around. Show students that you use the margins or sticky notes to add ideas in crucial areas. If you are lucky enough to have a large screen or projector hooked up to your computer, demonstrate how to use the tools from the word processor to make changes online. For example, in Microsoft Word, the reviewing tool bar will allow you to track the changes made from the original to the final copy. Positive comments can also be attached to the writing.

Share Revision Experiences and Tips from Other Writers

There are several helpful resources that share the perspective of authors of children's books and their experiences throughout the writing process, including revision. In the Meet the Author series, famous writers, including Eve Bunting and Patricia Polacco, address revision—their feelings about it, how they accomplish it, and tips for making it more effective. In *So, You Wanna Be a Writer?: How to Write, Get Published, and Maybe Even Make it Big!* by Vicki Hambleton, students receive different strategies for phase two of polishing their writing.

Tips from published writers can also be found on the Internet. At <www.Kids.Net.au>, your students can click on famous authors and receive a number of tips from revising to dealing with rejection as a writer. Jennie Shortridge has a page just for writers and provides several strategies for what she terms "intelligent revision." Taking time off between the first draft and subsequent drafts often allows students to see the writing in a more objective way.

Feature Writers in Your School

Ask successful writers in your school to share what they have learned about revision. Talk with teachers about students who show noticeable improvement from the first draft to the final copy. With very little time and expense, you can interview these writers at your school and ask them to share how they motivate themselves to stay with revision and decide what needs to be changed. The interviews should be taped and can be incorporated into a multimedia presentation that includes some of the students' published pieces as long as the necessary permissions have been obtained.

Share and Use Revision Checklists

Most students receive editing checklists from their teachers. In our experience, revision checklists are less common. If your school has a published English series, revision checklists for the different modes of writing are likely to be present in the textbooks and the additional resources. There are also several online resources that include revision checklists. Look for their addresses in the Works Consulted section at the end of this chapter.

Teachers who are very skilled at teaching writing may even construct revision checklists with their students as a summary of the writing lessons they have taught. This is a great form of review and makes expectations clear.

Engage in Interactive Revision

One of the most effective ways to engage students in revision is to get them to interact with their draft.

- Have the students locate elements in their piece that should be included:
  - *Sentence in which their message about the topic is stated or implied*
  - *Paragraph in which the problem or situation for the plot is first revealed*
  - *Main idea sentences that support the plot*
  - *Main events that continue or resolve the central problem or issue in the plot*
- Have students as they move into phase two of revision highlight examples of:
  - *Examples they have included to add clarity to their writing or a place where that is needed*
  - *Places where they have revealed a person's character through their actions or a place where that is needed*
  - *Examples of purposeful dialogue that advances the plot or understanding of a character or relationship or a place where that is appropriate*
  - *A place where a more precise term is used or needed*
- If students are working with organizational problems, making a reverse outline can be very effective. Have them list the message about the topic at the top of the paper. Moving through the piece, have them list the sentences that reveal the purpose for writing, main ideas, and concluding statements. If the piece is persuasive, listing the reasons will help them decide if they progress in order of importance.

Hold Revision Mini-Conferences

Conversations with students in small groups or individually when they are in the media center for five to 10 minutes will give writers a time to reflect on their ideas and to hear the questions from a fresh perspective. During these conversations your role is that of a listener. It is a good idea not to read their pieces, but to ask questions and then to listen to a section in the beginning, middle, or end that seems pertinent to their response or your question. Typical questions or prompts may include:

- Read the first part so that we can listen for your topic, purpose, and audience.
- What is your topic? What is your message about the topic? (expository)
- What is the plot? (narrative)
- Who is the major character? What do we discover about her/him? (narrative)
- Who is your audience for this piece?
- What can I do to help you?
- What would make your writing more interesting and clearer to your readers?
- Where does the piece need elaboration: examples, facts, comparisons?

- Locate one or more places where your information is clear and is quite easy to visualize.
- What will bother or confuse the reader? What questions will your reader still have? Are there gaps where the reader has to fill in missing information?
- Where might the reader lose interest?
- What needs to be cut?
- How satisfied are you with the introduction?
- Does each point or event lead to the next?
- Find a section where the writing moves too slowly.
- Are there sections where the writing moves too quickly?

Revisit Familiar Strategies from Prewriting and Drafting

When anchor papers are used along with drafting, they can be revisited to see how a particular writer framed his or her conclusion or made the dialogue interesting and purposeful. The entire paper does not need to be shown. Showing students one or more examples of effective introductions and discussing why each is effective will give them additional ideas for revising their own work.

Provide Teachers with Professional Materials

A display just on revision could include examples of first drafts and published forms discussed earlier. Here are several helpful books on writing that highlight the revision stage.

- *The Craft of Revision*, fourth edition, by Donald Murray is an excellent way to gain practical, in-depth understanding of revision.
- *Deep Revision* by Meredith Willis has many examples to use with students and library media specialists as well as teachers will find the "Try It Out" suggestions very practical.
- *Inside Writing* by Donald Graves and Penny Kittle contains a DVD of demonstration lessons and the text gives many ideas for teaching throughout the drafting and revision process.
- *Making Revision Matter* by Janet Angelillo suggests a revision unit of study where students learn more about the revision process and return to previous drafts to try out the strategies.
- *The Revision Toolbox* by Georgia Heard offers practical advice for students and their teachers in grades 3-8. It also includes focus lessons and samples of student writing.
- *Using Literature to Enhance Writing Instruction* by Rebecca Olness links lessons to literature that readers may already be familiar with. She examines what makes a particular book or section in a book so interesting or vivid. The same strategies can then be applied to revise student's own pieces.
- *Writing Reminders* by Jim Burke and The Reviser's Toolbox by Barry Lane are great resources for secondary teachers.

One More Thing...

Revision is essential to good writing. In this stage, the writer has the opportunity to refine his ideas to make the piece more interesting and clearer to his readers. By showing students how other writers made changes for their readers, students will come to appreciate the importance of revision. Revision does not have to be painful and should not involve recopying. By demonstrating simple and effective techniques for revision, the library media specialist will support writers and students in thinking of writing as communication.

Works Consulted

Burke, Jim. *Writing Reminders: Tools, Tips, and Techniques*. Portsmouth: Heinemann, 2003.

Graves, Donald, and Penny Kittle. *Inside Writing: How to Teach the Details of Craft*. Portsmouth: Heinemann, 2005.

Heard, Georia. *The Revision Toolbox: Teaching Techniques That Work*. Portsmouth: Heinemann, 2002.

Jennie Shortridge. 4 Jun. 2006. <www.jennieshortridge.com>.

Kids.Net.Au: Search Engine for Kids, Children, Parents, Educators, and Teachers. 4 Jun. 2006. <www.kids.net.au>.

Lane, Barry. *The Reviser's Toolbox*. Shoreham: Discover Writing Press, 1999.

Murray, Donald. *The Craft of Revision*. 4th ed. New York: Harcourt, 2004.

Olness, Rebecca. *Using Literature to Enhance Writing Instruction: A Guide for K-5 Teachers*. Newark: International Reading Association, 2005.

Willis, Meredith Sue. *Deep Revision: A Guide for Teachers, Students, and Other Writers*. New York: Teachers & Writers Collaborative, 2003.

Figure 6.1 Picture It
Library Media Center Collaboration Planning & Teaching Log

Teacher(s): _____
Grade Level: K-1_____ Planning Date: _____ Project Date: _____

Information Literacy Standards Standard 3	Academic Standards English/Language Arts
NETS Standards	**Essential Question** How do I use drawing to make my writing more interesting?

Picture It

Project Description:
30 minutes

Students will add details to something they have drawn to make it clearer and more interesting to their audience.

Sample Student Product

Original – I like to play ball after school.
Revised – When it is sunny, I like to play ball after school with my friend.

Teacher will: 2. Begin the lesson by having students draw something that they enjoy doing for fun after school. Allow about 10 minutes. Once they are finished, share a drawing from a student of the same grade. 3. Discuss the details they see in the picture relative to the setting and the emotions or actions that are present in the drawing. 6. Close the lesson by reminding students that each time they write something they will share with their audience, they should make changes to make it clearer and more interesting to their reader.	Library Media Specialist will: 1. Provide a picture that has been drawn by students of the same age and sample of student writing that includes a first draft and revision. 4. Tell students to make at least two revisions in their picture to help the other members of the class know the setting for the activity and who is with them. Link this to writing. 5. Read the first draft of the sample paper you selected. Solicit compliments from the students. Read the revision. Ask students to make compliments about the ways in which the revision is even clearer and more interesting.
Resources: Unlined paper and pencil	**Student Assessment:** Students will highlight one change they like in their writing. Teacher and LMS will check original drafts and revised drafts to see the changes that were made. **Project Evaluation:** Teacher and LMS will discuss additional times when students could revise their work.

Attach any other handouts, notes, or materials created for the project.

Figure 6.2 Great Beginnings
Library Media Center Collaboration Planning & Teaching Log

Teacher(s): _____
Grade Level: 2-5 _____ Planning Date: _____ Project Date:_____

Information Literacy Standards Standard 5	Academic Standards English/Language Arts
NETS Standards Standard 3	**Essential Question** How do I create a really good introduction?

Great Beginnings

Project Description:
Two 30 minutes sessions

Students will revise their writing by including or revising their introduction of expository text.

Sample Student Product

Original
The 500 mile race is run in Indiana over Memorial Day weekend. There are thirty-three cars in it. There is a parade in downtown Indianapolis the same weekend. Some people call this "the greatest spectacle in racing."

Revised
The sound of engines roars over the racetrack on Memorial Day weekend in Indiana. Racecar fans have already enjoyed a parade in downtown Indianapolis before the 33 cars line up for the "greatest spectacle in racing." Excitement flows through the veins of drivers and racecar fans as the race begins.

Teacher will:	**Library Media Specialist will:**
3. Have the students reread their first paragraph and decide if it is (1) a solid introduction, (2) is an introduction but needs to be revised to…, (3) is missing an introduction. 4. Call on several students to share their first paragraph and tell the class whether the first paragraph is a 1, 2, or 3. Ask their peers if they agree. 5. Plan on revisiting the first paragraphs the next day to revise and share the introductions.	1. Provide a sample of three or more introductions that are in the same mode of writing as the students are doing. 2. Begin by making the purpose of your lesson clear. Ask students to listen to the first paragraph of three pieces of writing. Ask them what all three have in common. Give them copies of the three introductory paragraphs. Guide them in seeing that in each introduction the writer's purpose is clear, attempts to engage the reader, and prompts them to keep reading.
Resources: Students will need the piece of writing they are working on and sticky notes.	**Student Assessment:** Students will put a plus by their favorite first paragraph. Teacher and LMS will check the first paragraphs on a rubric. Project Evaluation: Teacher and LMS will discuss how successful the introductions were with students and look for additional samples.

Attach any other handouts, notes, or materials created for the project.

Figure 6.3 Student Voice and Perspective
Library Media Center Collaboration Planning & Teaching Log

Teacher(s): _____
Grade Level: 6-8 _____ Planning Date: _____ Project Date:_____

Information Literacy Standards Standard 5 **NETS Standards** Standard 4	**Academic Standards** English/Language Arts Social Studies **Essential Question** How do I personalize my writing?

Student Voice and Perspective

Project Description:
Two 30 minute sessions

Students will experiment with voice to connect with their audience or to offer their own perspective on an issue.

Sample Student Product

Author's Voice	How Accomplished
Humorous	"The rocking chair tipped over and sent feathers a flying."
Serious	"It became clear from the data that the storm was coming."

Teacher will: 1. Begin by defining voice. Voice allows us to make a piece of writing uniquely ours by reflecting our perspective and personality. 3. Once students have a working understanding, take a second piece of writing and have them work along with others to decide how the second writer's voice is different from the first. Draw their attention to the list of characteristics you made for the first piece of writing. 4. Have students make two columns: descriptors of the author's voice and how he or she accomplishes it. If some students need additional support work along with them while others are more independent. Call on students to share one characteristic of voice and the technique used to accomplish it. Give the last two pieces of writing as an independent task. Give struggling students the more obvious of the two pieces.	**Library Media Specialist will:** 2. Provide students with four distinctive styles of writing. Advice columns, humorists, and political editorialists make excellent choices. Provide one example to all students and model how the voice of the writer becomes evident in what they say about the topic, the examples they use, the words and phrases that they choose to make the point, and the distance they place between themselves and the reader. Help them notice whether or not the writer is encouraging, telling, entertaining, criticizing, warning, etc. as the piece unfolds. 5. Suggest that they begin looking in the editorials. Extra credit could be given to students who bring in an example of voice from your local newspaper.
Resources: Four distinctive styles of writing.	**Student Assessment:** Students will reflect in one paragraph on how they created the voice for their writing. Teacher and LMS will check for consistency of voice. **Project Evaluation:** Teacher and LMS will discuss the writing styles used, how students reacted to them, and consider other examples.

Attach any other handouts, notes, or materials created for the project.

Figure 6.4 Character Revision
Library Media Center Collaboration Planning & Teaching Log

Teacher(s): _____
Grade Level: 9-12 _____ Planning Date: _____ Project Date: _____

Information Literacy Standards Standard 5 NETS Standards Standards 3 and 4	Academic Standards English/Language Arts Content Areas Essential Question How do I make my characters unique? Would my characters be more personalized if I changed their dialogue?

Character Revision

Project Description:
50 minutes

Students will revise a piece of their own writing by better defining a character or creating more personal dialogue.

Sample Student Product
Original
John said "I hope we win the ball game tomorrow."
"Do you think we have a chance?" said Mary.
"In sports, anything can happen," said John.
"You're right," said Mary.

Revised
John still dripped with sweat. He wiped his forehead and tried to catch his breath. "I hope we can win the ball game tomorrow. Winning the county championship would be a great way to finish my senior year." Mary skipped a few steps to catch up with John. Since she was almost a foot shorter than he, it was hard to match his long stride. "Do you think we have a chance?" she asked hesitantly. John closed his eyes briefly, looked to the sky, and replied, "In sports, anything can happen." Mary squeezed his arm and replied, "you're right."

Teacher will: Remind students of some ways to develop characters and dialogue. Assist students as they work on their individual writing.	Library Media Specialist will: Read aloud some sample quality dialogues from YA and adult literature. Assist students as they work on their individual writing.
Resources: Students' personal writing, computers, word processing software, paper, pencil	Student Assessment: Students will highlight their favorite dialogue passage and tell why they like it best. Teacher and LMS will include dialogue in their writing rubric and complete that segment. Project Evaluation: Teacher and LMS will discuss students' dialogue writing and look for additional sample literature.

Attach any other handouts, notes, or materials created for the project.

Chapter 7

Editing

> *Editing happens when the writer works on the mechanics or conventions of writing, such as punctuation, spelling, capitalization, or grammar.*
>
> *For many experienced teachers, childhood memories of writing include their teachers using a red pen to mark conventions mistakes on the papers. Little was said about revising for content. Drafts were edited for mechanics and then recopied for a "final" draft. Now we know that most editing should take place after revision that focused on creating clear content.*

As library media specialists, our role at this point takes two paths. We cautiously help teachers to distinguish between revising and editing, and we provide instructional support for the task. We assist students in finding resources that help them make correct choices in conventions and grammar.

Provide Teacher Assistance

As we pointed out in Chapter Three, you will need to balance your energy and enthusiasm for research and best practices with the realities of your current situation. Classroom teachers have often experienced minimal writing training in their educational courses. Their personal writing experiences may vary from using writing for correspondence to professionally published pieces. English teachers are usually very skilled in grammar conventions, but tend to teach them and assess them in isolation.

Many do not have a firm understanding of how to teach and manage editing within the writing process. It will be difficult for some teachers to admit this; others will freely state it. By sharing your own emerging understanding and providing information for teachers with article excerpts and your own highlighted notes, you can enhance understanding while keeping your working relationship intact. In some cases you will also be able to model for teachers if you ask to try out a focus lesson that you are excited about, such as teaching subject-verb agreement in the context of students' writing.

Order professional publications for your school that include writing information. List helpful Web sites on your library media center Web page or blog. Include books in your professional library that focus on good writing instruction. See the Works Consulted section of this chapter for suggested titles and sites.

After teachers have the information, we can assist them in using it with students. As library media specialists, we see numerous pieces of good literature. Offer to share some specific sections that represent particularly skilled use of sentence structure or paragraphing. Do lessons with the students that allow the classroom teacher to see you as a fellow instructor, not just a keeper of materials.

Provide Student Assistance

Students study English/language arts from kindergarten until they graduate from high school. However, some high school seniors still look confused over terms such as "adverbs" and "verbs" or they fail to use punctuation correctly. As library media specialists, we can help these students edit by showing them resources in our collection or Internet sources that can be used to assist them in editing.

Choose Words Carefully

Editing gives a chance to look at the entire document and use just the right words to create a document that furthers the author's purpose. Teenage writers get inspiration for writing and assistance on how to create better writing by reading books like the following titles.

- *Bird by Bird* makes readers laugh and tugs at their heart strings, while showing them how to improve their writing. They follow the author's writing process as she deals with a variety of events in her life.

- When they need to work on word choice, *Spunk & Bite and The Elements of Expression* also use humor to get serious information across to the reader. Neither of them needs to be read from the front cover to the back cover, but make great books to get nuggets of information.

- As teens polish their language usage, they may need something more than a thesaurus to be sure they have the right word. *Webster's Guide to English Usage* provides a quick reference for them.

Clarify Conventions

Conventions include the important segments of writing that are critical to how the piece looks. For example, grammar, punctuation, and capitalization affect whether or not the reader finds the piece easy to read or whether formatting issues distract from the writer's message. Check the Works Consulted section for Web sites and print materials that will assist you in helping students and staff know and apply correct conventions.

Correct Spelling

Provide a variety of dictionaries for your students. Marge remembers feeling frustrated as a child when she could not spell a word and then was told to look it up in the dictionary. At that point, you had to know how to spell it to look it up, so she never found that a satisfactory solution. Now, poor spellers have better options. Marge keeps an electronic dictionary in her desk and recommends that you make some available for your students. Sometimes her spelling is so poor, she has to try several different possibilities before she gets the right word, but it definitely works better than a standard print dictionary. She can usually recognize the correct word; she just has trouble spelling it independently. Put some picture dictionaries in your library media center. If you serve students who use a variety of languages, be sure to have dictionaries that represent those languages. Also keep an unabridged dictionary readily available in the library media center for those times when nothing else will show the word you want.

Word or vocabulary walls also help students with spelling and sometimes even word choice. Since library media centers serve multiple classes and grade levels, keeping those words current provides special challenges for library media specialists. Do change the words periodically to keep students interested. Try putting stars on the words of particular interest for a specific class.

Invented spelling, students writing a word as it sounds to them, comes up as a discussion topic in elementary schools. It allows students to share their thoughts, without the fear of spelling words incorrectly. The transfer from invented spelling to conventional spelling differs from school to school. Be sure you know your school's philosophy over whether or not it is acceptable. If so, know at what point students are expected to use conventional spelling.

Check Capitalization

Basic rules for capitalization are taught repeatedly in our country's school systems. However, questions occur as young writers develop their own work. Certainly, use the English/language arts textbook as a reference source. Be sure you have a copy of all textbooks in your facility. Having them there makes it easy for you to check information, and your teachers will appreciate having a copy available when they visit with their students. Also, in some schools, teachers can not stay in their classrooms during their preparation time, so they come to the library media center during that time. Having the textbooks in the library media center means teachers do not have to carry their copies from their classrooms.

Organize Paragraphing

Writers work to group appropriate sentences into paragraphs. Paragraphs provide proper divisions to help readers understand the text. Post Web sites on the library media center Web page that help students learn specifics on how to accomplish this task. Assist teachers with creating their own "help" sheets. Use already created information from Web sites listed in the Works Consulted section of this chapter.

Review Punctuation

Punctuation helps readers know how to pace reading of the text. Used well, it not only can add clarity but also can add drama! Help students see the importance of punctuation by displaying text from one of their favorite books without any punctuation. They will quickly see the importance of punctuation and then become more willing to learn how to apply it appropriately in their own writing.

Secondary teachers can spice up their teaching of punctuation by referring to *The New York Times* bestseller, *Eats, Shoots & Leaves*. This Britain's Book of the Year provides information in a humorous way, certain to entertain while informing. Teachers enjoy reading it and then sharing nuggets of text with their students. For a visual representation of the importance of commas, get the picture book *Eats, Shoots & Leaves: Why, Commas Really Do Make a Difference!* Each two-page spread shows the same sentence with the commas placed in different locations. The illustrations show how the comma placement changes the meaning of the text. Everyone who teaches comma use can enjoy using this picture book with their students.

Use Appropriate Grammar

In all the time we have been professional educators, none of us can remember one time when we have heard a teacher or a student express excitement about grammar. We think they just did not know about some of the wonderful trade literature that takes a dry subject and gives it new life. Look at the Literature Connections at the end of this chapter for specific titles. You can also find useful Web sites and Internet products that help writers edit their work. Check the Works Consulted section at the end of this chapter for specific Web addresses. When you share successful solutions with students and staff, they really appreciate your educational expertise as a library media specialist.

Apply Parts of Speech

Kindergarteners hear about the parts of speech, so it always amazes us when high school students still find the terms confusing. However, we know some do. Introducing any topic in its most basic format provides a good way to learn about it. We know elementary students like picture books, but do not hesitate to share some with high school students as well. They can appreciate them in ways that go right over the heads of elementary youth. We are fortunate to be teaching in a time when so many good books continue to be in print. Using those picture books and short chapter books to focus on parts of speech gives clarity to older students, who misunderstood the concepts. Check the Literature Connections section for specific titles. As library media specialists, we can lead the way in showing others the wealth of appropriate literature.

Examine Passive and Active Voice Verbs

When Marge first started writing a book review column for her local newspaper, she worked with a wonderful editor who offered to help improve her writing. Until that time, Marge's writing consisted of papers that she had written for college classes. Her goals had been to get good grades and have the correct number of pages. The newspaper editor wanted her to develop into a good writer.

One of the editor's first attempts involved helping Marge learn the difference between passive and active verbs. She told her to change to active voice verbs and Marge nodded at her in agreement, but it had been too long since Marge had heard those terms. She did not have a clue as to what the editor meant. She went to an elementary teacher who she was working with and asked for help. The teacher graciously reminded her of the definition of the terms and got her started moving from passive voice to active voice. Changing from passive to active voice made a world of difference in her writing. Later one of her bosses asked her to put "some exciting words" into his writing as she edited for him.

Students can see the difference between active and passive voice when given simple definitions. Active voice verbs "show," while passive voice verbs "tell." In active voice, the subject performs the verb action and the direct object receives it. For example, "Bill batted the ball." In passive voice, the object acts as the subject and includes a version of "to be." For example, "The ball was batted by Bill." To find passive voice and make it active voice, look for "is" or "was," and then make the appropriate changes to make it active voice.

Students can see a difference in their verb usage, if we help them. Try some of these techniques:

- Read aloud some favorite age-appropriate passages that represent active voice.
- With students, create a chart that shows sentences with both passive and active verbs.
- Model for students how to change a passive voice sentence to an active voice sentence.
- Provide a list of active verbs.
- Introduce students to Web sites that contain pages about verbs.

Eliminate Slang

Writers can use expressions and slang as a technique to help identify a time period or location. However, beginning writers may be so accustomed to the sound of slang that they do not realize what their use implies. Help students appreciate slang terms by making a list of terms from different eras. They will laugh at some of their parents' or grandparents' terms for expressing joy or disgust. Reference books that focus on idioms also give students an appreciative sense of language used in a variety of ways. See the Works Consulted section at the end of the chapter for specific titles.

Cite Sources

All writers need to acknowledge sources. The writers' ages dictate the details that should be included. High school English departments often choose a style to follow for their students. Adapting that style for younger students makes it easy for them to make the transition from simple styles to the complete style as a high school student. For a quick overview, keep copies of *A Pocket Style Manual* by Diana Hacker. The volume gives a summary of APA, Chicago, and MLA styles as well as information about grammar, punctuation, and mechanics. It gets updated periodically. For more details about the different styles, use APA, Chicago Manual of Style, and MLA Web sites.

Citing sources provides the perfect opportunity to emphasize the importance of avoiding plagiarism. Defining it for students in terms they understand provides the first step in preventing it. Young children understand the concept of taking something that does not belong to them. Explain to them that plagiarism is using someone else's ideas, without their permission or giving them credit. Older students find information about plagiarism at several of the Web sites at the end of this chapter. Some schools use software to search for plagiarized material. Turnitin.com provides that service as well as helpful information about plagiarism at <www.plagiarism.org>.

Offer Simple Solutions for Good Editing

Good editing means looking at the details in the writing. Editing should be one of the last steps in the writing process. The library media specialist can help staff and students through the process in the following ways.

- Use these editing ideas with teachers.
- Create an age/product appropriate checklist for students to use.
- Generate posters with students that represent the editing rules. Hang the posters prominently in the library media center or classrooms.
- Encourage peer-editing for beginning editing.
- Point out books or videos that include authors explaining their editing process.
- Offer to display edited work in the library media center, so students see it when they visit.

Try with students this handful of ideas to check for editing concerns.

- Read aloud slowly, so you actually read the word you wrote, not the one you meant to write.
- Check for subject/verb agreement.
- Check for consistency in verb tense.
- Look for appropriate capitalization and punctuation.
- Examine the paragraphs to see if they include enough details for the reader to understand your intention as the writer.

One More Thing…

Editing makes writing easier to read. It allows writers to polish their work to mechanical perfection after revising the ideas. As library media specialists, we assist in this step of the process by providing reference sources and helping students use the appropriate tools.

Literature Connections

Cleary, Brian. *Dearly, Nearly, Insincerely: What Is an Adverb?* Minneapolis: Lerner Publications, 2005.

Cleary, Brian. *Hairy, Scary, Ordinary: What Is an Adjective?* Minneapolis: First Avenue Editions, 2001.

Cleary, Brian. *How Much Can a Bare Bear Bear?: What Are Homonyms and Homophones?* Minneapolis: Millbrook Press, 2005.

Cleary, Brian. *I and You and Don't Forget Who: What Is a Pronoun?* Minneapolis: Carolrhoda Books, 2004.

Cleary, Brian. *A Lime, a Mime, a Pool of Slime: More about Nouns.* Minneapolis, Millbrook Press, 2006.

Cleary, Brian. *Mink, a Fink, a Skating Rink: What Is a Noun?* Minneapolis: Carolrhoda Books, 1999.

Cleary, Brian. *Pitch and Throw, Grasp and Know: What Is a Synonym?* Minneapolis: Carolrhoda Books, 2004.

Cleary, Brian. *Stop and Go, Yes and No: What Is an Antonym?* Minneapolis: Millbrook Press, 2006.

Cleary, Brian. *To Root, to Toot, to Parachute: What Is a Verb?* Minneapolis: Carolrhoda Books, 2001.

Cleary, Brian. *Under, Over, by the Clover: What Is a Preposition?* Minneapolis: Carolrhoda Books, 2003.

Heller, Ruth. *Behind the Mask: A Book about Prepositions.* New York: Putnam Juvenile; Reprint edition, 1998.

Heller, Ruth. *A Cache of Jewels: and Other Collective Nouns.* New York: Putnam Juvenile, 1998.

Heller, Ruth. *Fantastic! Wow! and Unreal!: A Book about Interjections and Conjunctions.* New York: Putnam Juvenile, 2000.

Heller, Ruth. *Kites Sail High: A Book about Verbs.* New York: Putnam Juvenile; Reissue edition, 1998.

Heller, Ruth. *Many Luscious Lollipops: A Book about Adjectives.* New York: Putnam Juvenile; Reissue edition, 1998.

Heller, Ruth. *Merry-Go-Round: A Book about Nouns.* New York: Putnam Juvenile; Reissue edition, 1998.

Heller, Ruth. *Mine, All Mine: A Book about Pronouns.* New York: Putnam Juvenile; Reprint edition, 1999.

Heller, Ruth. *Up, Up and Away: A Book about Adverbs.* New York: Putnam Juvenile; Reissue edition, 1998.

Lamott, Anne. *Bird by Bird.* New York: Anchor Books, 1995.

Plotnik, Arthur. *The Elements of Expression.* New York: Barnes & Noble, 1996, 2006.

Plotnik, Arthur. *Spunk & Bite.* New York: Random House Reference, 2005.

Pulver, Robin. *Nouns and Verbs Have a Field Day.* New York: Holiday House, 2006.

Pulver, Robin. *Punctuation Takes a Vacation.* New York: Holiday House, 2003.

Terban, Marvin. *Building Your Vocabulary and Making It Great!* New York: Scholastic, 2003.

Terban, Marvin. *Checking Your Grammar.* New York: Scholastic Reference, 1994.

Terban, Marvin. *Guppies in Tuxedos: Funny Eponyms.* New York: Clarion Books, 1988.

Terban, Marvin. *I Think I Thought: and Other Tricky Verbs.* New York: Clarion Books, 1984.

Terban, Marvin. *In a Pickle and Other Funny Idioms.* New York: Clarion Books, 1983.

Terban, Marvin. *It Figures!: Fun Figures of Speech.* New York: Clarion Books, 1993.

Terban, Marvin. *Mad as a Wet Hen!: and Other Funny Idioms.* New York: Clarion Books, 1987.

Terban, Marvin. *Punching the Clock: Funny Action Idioms.* New York: Clarion Books, 1990.

Terban, Marvin. *Punctuation Power: Punctuation and How to Use It*. New York: Scholastic Reference; Reprint edition, 2002.

Terban, Marvin. *Scholastic Writer's Desk Reference*. New York: Scholastic Reference, 2001.

Terban, Marvin. *Time to Rhyme: A Rhyming Dictionary*. Honesdale: Boyds Mills Press; Reprint edition, 1997.

Terban, Marvin. *Verbs! Verbs! Verbs!* New York: Scholastic Reference, 2002.

Terban, Marvin. *Your Foot's on My Feet: and Other Tricky Nouns*. New York: Clarion Books, 1986.

Truss, Lynne. *Eats, Shoots & Leaves: Why, Commas Really Do Make a Difference!* New York: G.P. Putnam's Sons, 2006.

Webster's Guide to English Usage. New York: Barnes & Noble, 2004.

Works Consulted

Ammer, Christine. *The American Heritage Dictionary of Idioms: The Most Comprehensive Collection of Idiomatic Expressions and Phrases*. New York: Houghton Mifflin, 2003.

APA Style. *American Psychological Association*. 4 Jun. 2006. <www.apastyle.org>.

Bellamy, Peter. *Seeing with New Eyes*. 6th ed. North West Regional Educational Laboratory, 2005.

Calkins, Lucy. *The Art of Teaching Writing*. 2nd ed. New York: Heinemann, 1994.

Chicago Style Q&A: Documentation. The University of Chicago. 4 Jun. 2006. <www.chicagomanualofstyle.org/cmosfaq.html>.

Hacker, Diana. *A Pocket Style Manual*. New York: Bedford/St. Martins, 2006.

The International Reading Association. 4 Jun. 2006. <www.reading.org>.

Journal of Teaching Writing Profiles. 6 Jul. 2005. Indiana University-Purdue University Indianapolis. 4 Jun. 2006. <www.iupui.edu/~jtw/profiles.htm>.

Laurier Writing Centre Handouts. 2006. Wilfrid Laurier University. 4 Jun. 2006. <info.wlu.ca/writing/handouts.shtml>.

Modern Language Association. 4 Jun. 2006. <www.mla.org>.

The National Council of Teachers of English. 4 Jun. 2006. <www.ncte.org>.

National Writing Project. 4 Jun. 2006. <www.writingproject.org/About/map.csp>.

New York University Punctuation. 31. Jan. 2005. Sonia Jaffe Robbins. 4 Jun. 2006. <www.nyu.edu/classes/copyXediting/Punctuation.html>.

North Carolina State University's Online Writing Lab. 4 Jun. 2006. <http://www2.ncsu.edu:8010/ncsu/grammar>.

Plagiarism.org. iParadigms, LLC. 21 Jul. 2006. <www.plagiarism.org>.

Plot, Arthur. Spunk & Bite. New York: Random House Reference, 2005.

Punctuation Made Simple. Gary A. Olson. The College of Arts & Sciences at Illinois State University. 4 Jun. 2006. <lilt.ilstu.edu/golson/punctuation>.

Punctuation Marks. Capital Community College Foundation. 4 Jun. 2006.

<grammar.ccc.commnet.edu/grammar/marks/marks.htm>.

Purdue University's Online Writing Lab. The Writing Lab & The OWL at Purdue and Purdue University. 4 Jun. 2006. <owl.english.purdue.edu>.

Read Write Think. IRA/NCTE. 4 Jun. 2006. <www.readwritethink.org>.

Rodgers, James. *The Dictionary of Clichés*. New York: Barnes and Noble Books, 2001.

Spears, Richard. *NTC's Dictionary of American Slang and Colloquial Expressions*. New York: McGraw Hill, 1999.

Teaching PreK-8: The Magazine for Professional Development. Teaching PreK-8. 4 Jun. 2006. <www.teachingk-8.com>.

Truss, Lynne. Eats, Shoots & Leaves. New York: Penguin, 2003.

University of Colorado Style Guide. 2002. Regents of the University of Colorado. 4 Jun. 2006. <www.colorado.edu/Publications/styleguide/index.html>.

University of North Carolina at Chapel Hill Writing Center Handouts. 18 Jul. 2006. UNC-CH Writing Center. 30 Sep. 2006. <www.unc.edu/depts/wcweb/handouts.html>.

University of Saskatchewan's Language Center Helpful ESL Links. 5 Nov. 2005. Dewey Litwiller. 4 Jun. 2006. <http://homepage.usask.ca/~dul381/common/helpfulesllinks.html>.

University of Washington's Bothell Writing Center Resources. 1 Sept. 2006. 30 Sep. 2006. <http://www.uwb.edu/writingcenter/resources.xhtml>.

Figure 7.1 Spelling Words Wall
Library Media Center Collaboration Planning & Teaching Log

Teacher(s): _____
Grade Level: K-1 _____ Planning Date: _____ Project Date: _____

Information Literacy Standards Standard 3	Academic Standards English/Language Arts
NETS Standards Standard 3	Essential Question When I write, do I use invented spelling? Can I find help to spell a word conventionally?

Spelling Word Walls

Project Description:
15 minutes

Students will know resources to use that give conventional spelling.

Sample Student Project

Students double check spelling in their personal writing.

Original
My dog is smal. His name is Ruff. We play catsh every day. He is my god fren.

Revised
My dog is small. His name is Ruff. We play catch every day. He is my good friend.

Teacher will: Post most used words on classroom wall. Define invented and conventional spelling. Model using invented spelling. Assist students as they work on using conventional spelling.	Library Media Specialist will: Post most used words on LMC wall. Purchase picture dictionaries. Teach how to use a picture dictionary. Assist students as they work on using conventional spelling.
Resources: Picture dictionaries Word walls Student writing	**Student Assessment:** Students will highlight words they changed. Teacher and LMS will check spelling on final draft writing. **Project Evaluation:** Teacher and LMS will talk about age-appropriate spelling and additional resources to support spelling.

Attach any other handouts, notes, or materials created for the project.

Figure 7.2 Parts of Speech
Library Media Center Collaboration Planning & Teaching Log

Teacher(s): _____
Grade Level: 2-5 _____   Planning Date: _____   Project Date: _____

Information Literacy Standards Standard 3 NETS Standards Standard 4	Academic Standards English/Language Arts Essential Question Do I understand the parts of speech and can I create a poster that represents that knowledge?

Parts of Speech

Project Description:
30 minutes

Students will better understand the parts of speech, e.g., noun, pronoun, adjective, adverb, preposition, conjunction, and interjection

Sample Student Project
Students will create posters representing the parts of speech.

Teacher will: Direct students to draw pictures or cut out appropriate ones from magazines that represent the parts of speech. Hang posters in the classrooms.	Library Media Specialist will: Create model poster. Read aloud one of the books that focuses on the parts of speech. See Chapter Seven Literature Connections. Provide resources. Demo how to use the drawing software.
Resources: See Chapter Seven Literature Connections Paper, magazine pictures, glue sticks, crayons, drawing software	Student Assessment: Students will double-check their personal poster against a model poster. Teacher and LMS will create checklist and fill it out for students. Project Evaluation: Teacher and LMS will discuss the project and listen/look for students' proper use of parts of speech.

Attach any other handouts, notes, or materials created for the project.

Editing

Figure 7.3 Active and Passive Voice
Library Media Center Collaboration Planning & Teaching Log

Teacher(s): _____
Grade Level: 6-8 _____ Planning Date: _____ Project Date: _____

Information Literacy Standards Standard 3 NETS Standards Standard 4	Academic Standards English/Language Arts Essential Question Do I recognize passive voice? Do I know how to change it?

Active and Passive Voice

Project Description:
30 minutes

Students will change their own writing from passive to active voice.

Sample Student Project

Passive Voice
The fire truck was racing through the street and the group of boys heard it. The siren was very loud. The boys wondered where the truck was going.

Active Voice
The group of boys heard the fire truck racing through the street. They listened to the loud siren and wondered about the truck's target location.

Teacher will: Define active and passive voice to students. Instruct the students to change a piece of their own writing from passive to active voice. Assist students in editing their writing.	**Library Media Specialist will:** Model changing writing from passive to active voice on a personal writing sample. Teach how to use appropriate word processing features, e.g., track changes, comments, etc. Assist students in editing their writing.
Resources: Sample LMS' writing Students' writing Word processing software, pencil and paper	**Student Assessment:** Students will highlight their active voice verbs. Teacher and LMS will check students' writing. **Project Evaluation:** Teacher and LMS will discuss the project and listen/look for students' proper use of active voice.

Attach any other handouts, notes, or materials created for the project.

Figure 7.4 Connecting Language to the Time Period
Library Media Center Collaboration Planning & Teaching Log

Teacher(s): _____
Grade Level: 9-12 _____ Planning Date: _____ Project Date: _____

Information Literacy Standards Standard 5 NETS Standards Standard 4	Academic Standards English/Language Arts Social Studies Essential Question How does language from another time period compare to current expressions?

Connecting Language to the Time Period

Project Description:
120 minutes

Students will choose a decade and find words that were used during that time period.

Sample Student Product

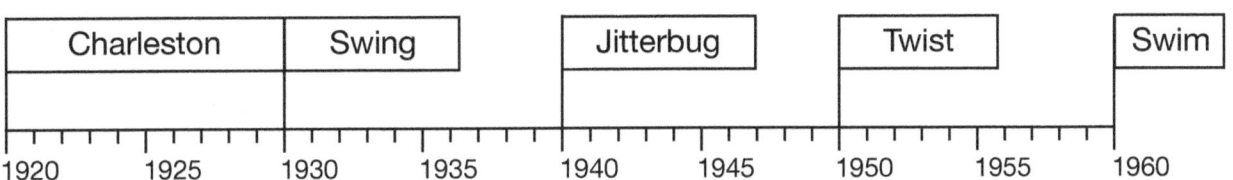

Teacher will: Show segments of videos representing different time periods. Suggest interviewing people who remember other decades. Talk about the words that all will look for, i.e. describing pleasure, disgust, dances, etc. Direct students to choose a decade of interest. Assist students as they add words to the timeline.	Library Media Specialist will: Provide reference materials and instruction on how to locate sources representing specific time periods. Demo how to create a timeline using the preferred software. Assist students as they add words to the timeline. Display products in the LMC.
Resources: Word processing or Timeliner software	Student Assessment: Students will respond to rubric created by teacher and LMS. Teacher and LMS will respond to their created rubric. Project Evaluation: Teacher and LMS will reflect on the experience and look for additional sources.

Attach any other handouts, notes, or materials created for the project.

Chapter 8

Publishing

> ***Publishing is the act of sharing a piece of
> writing with the intended audience.***
>
> ***While not all pieces are going to make it to the publishing stage, publishing is the
> pay off for all of a writer's hard work. Sharing one's ideas with the audience and
> getting feedback is critical. It is not until the writer receives feedback from the
> intended audience that the process has concluded.***

Writers have many options and methods for sharing their ideas with others. Technology has expanded the possibilities beyond the traditional report and oral presentation in front of the class. Multimedia presentations, Web sites, video production, electronic bulletin boards, and other forms of e-publishing open the doors for more and faster feedback for writers. By making students aware of their choices and fostering publication throughout the school, the library media specialist gives writers the tools and opportunities they need to continue to want to write.

Options for Publishing

As during all the stages in writing, focusing on the audience of the intended piece will suggest how the piece might be published. The format chosen can enhance the message and foster greater interest from the reader.

Printing

Even when teachers or students choose a report format, there are many ways to modify or change the information into something more appealing for all. Variations might include a brochure, a memo to the principal to share the information the writer learned, or the class might decide to publish a newspaper in which each student writes an article about the topic on a different aspect or from a different point of view.

You might try publishing greeting cards with students. This provides a relatively quick exposure to the writing process and allows for individualized student expression. The experience ties to social studies standards, as students discover holidays celebrated in different parts of the world. It also makes a good tie to visual arts standards. The prewrite includes basic cultural research as well as discussion of cards students give and receive. Students draft a card of their choice. They share it with at least one other person to get some revision ideas. They make changes; of course, after that they check for editing issues. The final product can be displayed, but eventually it goes to a specific recipient. Marge utilized this learning experience with several different groups of students and found it played out successfully, regardless of their ages.

Speaking

The standards for English/language arts in many states provide for oral speaking standards. Students are required to speak in front of an audience. The writing process can provide abundant opportunities for public speaking from informally sharing the writing in a group to organizing and writing a coherent and well-developed speech. Through multiple opportunities for public speaking, students gain confidence by sharing something they know well. When the writer speaks from a position of authority and personal interest, it is easier to make and maintain eye contact and to connect with the audience. Many schools—especially at the high school level—provide public forums for sharing poetry and other student writing. The public library in the community where Carl and Marge work offers a poetry contest opportunity to all secondary students in the county. Check with your local public library to see if a collaborative opportunity exists. Elementary schools may give students the opportunity to read something they wrote over the morning announcements. Smaller audiences are made available through use of an author's chair in the classroom.

Visual

Computer slides, such as PowerPoint, are a great replacement for note cards. Depending on the time and complexity of the presentation, simple key points or more elaborate video clips can be incorporated to guide the writer through the presentation and enhance his message.

Students may also format their writing as a narrative for a video or a script for actors to perform as a play. This shift provides a greater challenge for students than writing a typical report. It also demonstrates the power of writing in shaping the actions of others, as writers see the video they have narrated played before a live audience or watch a performance of a skit they have created. Video can also record a student reading his writing and can be used for self-evaluation of both speaking and writing standards. When a writer plays back the tape, he hears the piece as it sounds to others and may catch elements that will cause him to revise or edit.

Software programs such as Kidspiration and Inspiration, while often thought of as part of the prewrite step, can also be used for students to create a final product to share their information.

Web Opportunities

Web pages are another format for students to share their information with the world. Posting work on a school Web site can help provide the students with another outlet for sharing their writing. The use of the Internet is an obvious way to find new audiences for writing and to share ideas with readers beyond the school. Besides publishing on the school Web site, many Web sites and services are available that will publish students work online. As with all outside groups, it is important that you investigate and make sure the site is safe, appropriate, and legitimate. Students enjoy seeing their work posted and many of these sites have samples of other student writing.

Publishing on the Web changes the student's audience, so it too will alter what will be included in the piece. Obviously there are safety concerns with posting information on the Internet, and children should never put up personal information or contact information. But, through the Web, grandma and grandpa, who live 1,000 miles away, could view the writing and enjoy seeing their grandchildren's successes. As with all creative works, the copyright for a student's material remains with the student. You will want to make sure to get their permission (along with parental consent) before posting any writing online.

At the end of this chapter in our Works Consulted section, you will find some links to information about posting student writing online.

Provide Teacher Assistance

Publishing, along with prewriting, is one of the easiest steps in the writing process in which to begin collaboration. With the explosion of technology available in the last decade, the library media specialist can be a vital resource for sharing emerging technologies by staying up-to-date through her own research and seeking out teachers who delight in technology. Sharing new options for publishing and demonstrating its use is an obvious way to expand our instructional role. As leaders in technology, this provides an obvious connection to classroom teachers and collaborative experiences. Teachers will welcome ideas and support the development of final projects that go beyond the typed report. Instructing students on using technology and providing another pair of hands when students work in groups leads towards more sophisticated and terrific final projects.

Provide Student Assistance

Since publishing is also the last step in the process, it provides us with another opportunity to remind students about intellectual property and the copyright issues involved. We can help them to ensure that they have properly cited all the sources they used to compile their information. When students are creating fictional writing, we can help them to think about their copyright, too. The focus shifts from citing sources to how their work is protected from others using it without their permission.

The library media center can provide examples of other final projects in display cases and on the tops of book cases. When asked, students often donate their materials to the collection upon completion of the project. Future students appreciate seeing teachers' expectations as they begin and continue their work. Beginning in the primary grades, books created by the entire class make great donations to the school library. Marge used those opportunities to explain how cataloging entries were created for those local books. The students were always excited to see their book appearing in the same automation system as their favorite authors. It also made cataloging make more sense to students.

Planning the Delivery and Presentation

As students use technology to support their presentations, they will need you to teach or remind them that technology should enhance the message, not compete for the audience's attention. There is a delicate balance between finding the right tool to use at the right time and using technology just because it exists. We can model how to integrate technology to connect with our audience by:

- Using a less is more approach to technology and varying the presentation style across the year.
- Using a minimum of 18 point type to make the text readable.
- Using a consistent theme or design throughout the presentation for consistency.
- Thinking carefully about how much text is needed in support of the oral presentation. Six lines of text per slide is the norm. Show students how to distill their information to just enough on the screen to remind people where you are in the presentation and what the key ideas are.

One More Thing...

Publishing is a perfect place for collaborative connections. Teachers appreciate new ideas for using technology and providing students with options and choices. This is a perfect place for library media specialists to be available to help students and teachers in finding the perfect medium and format for sharing their writing.

Literature Connections

Carter, David, and James R. Diaz. *Let's Make It Pop-Up*. New York: Simon & Schuster, 2004.

Christelow, Eileen. *What Do Authors Do?* New York: Clarion Books, 1995.

Christelow, Eileen. *What Do Illustrators Do?* New York: Clarion Books, 1999.

Irvine, Joan. *Easy to Make Pop-Ups*. Dover Publications, 2005.

Irvine, Joan. *How to Make Holiday Pop-Ups*. New York: William Morrow, 1996.

Leedy, Loreen. *Look at My Book*. New York: Holiday House, 2004.

Rylant, Cynthia. Mr. *Putter & Tabby Write the Book*. New York: Harcourt, 2004.

Valenta, Barbara. *Pop-O-Mania: How to Create Your Own Pop-Ups*. New York: Penguin, 1997.

Works Consulted

Meryln's Pen. 2006. Merlyn's Pen Foundation. 11 Jun. 2006. <www.merlynspen.org>.

Payton, Tammy. "Empowering Student Learning with Web Publishing." 11 Jun. 2006. <www.siec.k12.in.us/~west/article/publish.htm>.

Stone Soup. 11 Jun. 2006. <www.stonesoup.com>.

Figure 8.1 Drawing
Library Media Center Collaboration Planning & Teaching Log

Teacher(s): _____
Grade Level: K-1 _____ Planning Date: _____ Project Date: _____

Information Literacy Standards Standard 3 NETS Standards Standards 3 and 4	Academic Standards English/Language Arts Fine Arts Essential Question Which of my written ideas do I try to put into pictures?

Drawing

Project Description:
30 minutes

Students will illustrate a picture, using software, to accompany their writing.

Sample Student Product

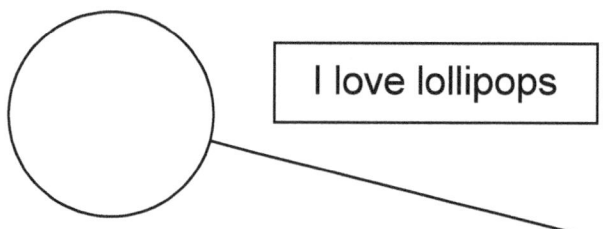

Teacher will: Help students revise/edit writing as needed. Help students produce a finished piece of writing. Assist students in entering artwork into the computer.	**Library Media Specialist will:** Help students revise/edit writing as needed. Lead instruction in the computer lab using Kid Pix or other drawing software. Assist students in entering artwork into the computer.
Resources: Kid Pix Drawing program in word processing program Student writing	**Student Assessment:** Students will + or – how they feel about how their drawing supports their writing. Teacher will assess student writing use a rubric. LMS will make observations about students comfort levels with a mouse. **Project Evaluation:** Teacher and LMS will meet to evaluate this project and make suggestions for the next time.

Attach any other handouts, notes, or materials created for the project.

Figure 8.2 Brochures
Library Media Center Collaboration Planning & Teaching Log

Teacher(s): _____
Grade Level: 2-5 _____ Planning Date: _____ Project Date: _____

Information Literacy Standards Standard 6 NETS Standards Standards 3 and 4	Academic Standards English/Language Arts Content Area Essential Question How do I create a brochure that informs and interests the audience?

Brochures

Project Description:
Three 30 minutes sessions

Students will create a brochure based on curriculum content such as animal information, specific states or countries, etc.

Sample Student Product

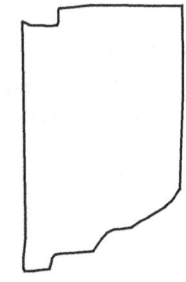

Indiana

The Hoosier State

My Favorite Fact:
They grow popcorn.

Teacher will: Assign students a research topic that allows students some choice in the content. Help students revise/edit writing as needed. Help students produce a finished piece of writing.	Library Media Specialist will: Assist students with appropriate resources. Help students revise/edit writing as needed. Lead instruction in the computer lab using word processing software to create brochures.
Resources: Curriculum content resources Word processing software	Student Assessment: Students will check off assignment expectations. Teacher and LMS will assess the brochure using a rubric that reflects content as well as technical abilities. Project Evaluation: Teacher and LMS will meet to evaluate this project and make suggestions for the next time.

Attach any other handouts, notes, or materials created for the project.

Figure 8.3 *Scripting*
Library Media Center Collaboration Planning & Teaching Log

Teacher(s): _____
Grade Level: 6-8 _____ Planning Date: _____ Project Date: _____

Information Literacy Standards Standard 6 NETS Standards Standard 4	Academic Standards English/Language Arts Content Areas Essential Question What do I feel passionately about that I want to tell my views to others?

Scripting

Project Description:
Four 45 minute time periods

Students will make a video to convey a message to the intended audience.

Sample Student Product
                    Water, Water Everywhere, But Not a Drop to Drink
                                    Science Video

Shot	Text
Local river with recreational users	Blue River flows through our county. It provides a place to swim and fish.
Local industry buildings	Unfortunately, it also provides a dumping spot for local industries.
Glass of water clearly fading to cloudy water	What do you want to drink?

Teacher will: Help guide students with writing. Students work to create a script that not only gives the characters their voice, but also their actions and feelings. Help students divide writing into storyboards. Help students focus on the audience. Just as a piece of writing has an audience and a message to convey, so does the video. How are they different? Same?	**Library Media Specialist will:** Help students divide writing into storyboards. Students will use a storyboard to divide their written script into scenes. This will provide guidance while filming. This step could also be done before writing of the script as a pre-write exercise. Provide guidance while filming and editing the video. Students film the video. They may use editing software such as iMovie.
Resources: Paper Pencil Storyboard iMovie or other editing software Camcorder	**Student Assessment:** Student will use a checklist during the process. Using a rubric, the teacher will assess students on the written script and convey a message to the audience. LMS will assess students using a rubric on the video production and how they conveyed a message to the audience. **Project Evaluation:** The LMS and teacher will meet to evaluate the project for future collaborations.

Attach any other handouts, notes, or materials created for the project.

The Library Media Specialist in the Writing Process

Figure 8.4 Web Page
Library Media Center Collaboration Planning & Teaching Log

Teacher(s): _____
Grade Level: 9-12 _____ Planning Date: _____ Project Date: _____

Information Literacy Standards Standards 6, 7, and 8 NETS Standards Standards 3 and 4	Academic Standards English/Language Arts Content Area Essential Question What do I know enough about that I can use to create a Web page that informs and interests the audience?

Web Page

Project Description:
Four 30 minutes sessions

Students will create a Web page based on curriculum content in which they are interested.

Sample Student Product

Healthy Eating + Consistent Exercise = Quality Life

Local news reports say American teens weigh in the obese levels and don't exercise enough. This interests me, because my brother, John, was just diagnosed with type 2 diabetes and the doctor said John's weight was a big issue with his diabetes. Teens want more from life than snack food and computer games. Check out the following Web sites to find out about good eating facts and exercise to keep you moving.

<u>**Good Eating Facts**</u>   <u>**Exercise**</u>

Teacher will: Assign students to research a topic of interest and create a Web page as a final project. Help students revise/edit writing as needed. Help students produce a finished piece of writing.	**Library Media Specialist will:** Assist students in researching information. Help students revise/edit writing as needed. Lead instruction in the computer lab on how to create a Web page.
Resources: Curriculum content resources Web page creation software	**Student Assessment:** Students will use a rubric for a self assessment. Teacher and LMS will assess with a rubric a student Web page. **Project Evaluation:** Teacher and LMS will meet to evaluate this project and make suggestions for the next time.

Attach any other handouts, notes, or materials created for the project.

Publishing 109

Chapter 9

Response to Writing

> *Response is a reaction to what has been written.*
> *Response to writing can be everything from a smile to formal evaluation.*
> *In real life, the response we receive is dependent on the audience and purpose for writing.*

All of us have received responses to our writing. When Susan was nine, she wrote a letter to "Betty Crocker" explaining that one of her advertisements on television used ungrammatical language. The advertisement claimed that the new and improved cake recipe was moister than its predecessor. In her letter, Susan politely explained that there was no such word as "moister," with the correct phrase being "more moist." The response from the company was courteous and warm, and they said that in advertising it is sometimes fun and effective to coin new phrases to get people's attention. Had the company decided not to write back, it might have taken Susan longer to appreciate the power of the pen, and today, she might be buying someone else's cake mixes.

For purposes of clarity in this chapter we have divided responses to writing into two categories: informal feedback and formal evaluation. In both cases, as you read in Chapter One, the response should be clear, specific, and generally positive. Here we will explore ways that you can work along with teachers to respond to writing effectively and efficiently.

Informal Feedback

Feedback to writing occurs when one or more people share their thoughts about the quality of the writing in its present form. Feedback can be given to the writer by discussing the writing in a conference, sharing comments, responding to items on a list of criteria, and even asking questions. The type and amount of feedback will influence the quality of students' writing, their motivation to continue to write, and their desire to write well.

One of the most important ways to work together to support writers is to decide the focus of the writing feedback for students. If the students are working on personal narratives, brainstorm one or two traits or qualities that are most important for students to understand and use in their personal narratives. Perhaps writers should concentrate on precise words and examples to create powerful images for their readers. When educators use shared criteria, their feedback to writers is more consistent and therefore, more powerful.

Feedback is especially helpful when the writer solicits feedback and expects to use it to revise or edit. In *The Craft of Revision,* Donald Murray refers to these as "test readers." Their job is to respond to the draft in its current form, without explanation from the writer. As Marge, Carl, and Susan began the process of writing this book, they received early feedback from reviewers provided by their publisher. While all three authors knew the manuscript was very rough and would need extensive rewriting and editing, they waited eagerly for the response. The feedback was extremely helpful in terms of the overall quality of the writing, but there were a few comments about the usefulness of the information for busy library media specialists. Therefore, the authors solicited the response of two colleagues who were retired library media specialists. As soon as their feedback arrived, Marge, Carl, and Susan plunged in eagerly to revise and continue writing. In all cases, the feedback was extremely helpful and powerful in shaping this book because it was direct but not harsh, very specific, and the authors expected to use it.

As you work with the teachers in your building you might begin with a discussion of why writers need, and should use, feedback. Begin by having each educator share how writing feedback may hurt a little, but when used, makes the piece so much better. If you do not already have examples to share, you can begin by asking your students for feedback on a current piece of yours. They will learn through your examples that early and continued feedback improves the quality of writing for the intended audience. When you are fortunate enough to have visiting authors in your school or school corporation, ask the organizer of the event if they will ask the guest author to include a few comments about the importance of asking for and using feedback. Most children's and young adults' authors are very happy to speak to the topic when asked.

Feedback is even more useful when the writer tells what kind of feedback is needed. The writing traits can be helpful in framing the type of response that is needed. Show your students how to ask for specific feedback by picking one aspect for attention. Perhaps the writer is struggling with the organization of the piece or needs suggestions of more precise words to strengthen the message. When Marge, Carl, and Susan sent their manuscript to the library media specialists, they asked for feedback on voice and found it useful.

Young or inexperienced writers may not know what kind of help they need. Until they know more about the qualities of good writing and have a solid understanding of focus or a clear message, the educators can decide what the focus should be. Susan usually begins by teaching students of all ages that their writing should have a clear message and answer her most consistent question, "What is the one thing you want your reader to know, understand, or believe about your topic?" Correspondingly, on the first draft, she gives feedback on whether or not there is a message and whether or not it is clear.

Walking Feedback

In the 1980's, the term MBWA, management by walking around, referred to a style where managers interacted with their staff as they worked. The same concept works as students are engaged in the writing process. In library media centers and classrooms, teachers and library media specialists can circulate as students work, give specific feedback, affirm student's efforts, and facilitate problem solving. The classroom teacher may zero in on three or four things while the library media specialist may concentrate her effort on one item. For example, the classroom teacher may be circulating and making comments or raising questions about the effective use of dialogue, use of comparisons and analogies, and transitions among paragraphs if they have been the subject of recent focus lessons. You can circulate as students work and comment solely on the use of dialogue to reveal character traits, pulling helpful examples from books within the media center.

Writing Conferences

A conference is a conversation between the writer and one or more individuals about the piece of writing or how the student works as a writer. In secondary classrooms, writing conferences are difficult to manage but equally important. Teachers accomplish them by using a combination of peer and teacher conferences simultaneously. The student(s) not involved in a conference with the teacher are conferring with one another, using the established procedures and norms. In effective conferences, the writer does more talking than the audience or teacher. The listeners pay careful attention to what the writer is saying or trying to say. Wait time is important. Students are encouraged to share what is working and not working and to ask for help. Those giving feedback ask questions, make comments, and avoid critical, judgmental language. In an effective conference, the writer emerges more motivated and has a clear direction of what to do or try next.

For the library media specialist, conferences happen more on a "need some help" basis. Writers may solicit feedback or ask you to help solve a problem. A common one is "I can not figure out what to say next." With a good understanding of the writing process and the expectations of the student's teacher, you can provide an amazing amount of information in a very short time by thoughtful questioning.

- What specific problem are you trying to solve?
- What is your topic and message?
- What are the main points you have made so far?
- Do you have a project checklist and/or a rubric?
- How long did you prewrite?
- What have you tried to solve the problem?
- What feedback have you received so far from teachers and peers?

Showing students examples of a published piece that has the qualities they are trying to create in their own writing is one of the most effective ways to conclude a quick conference.

Written Feedback

In several schools where Marge, Carl, and Susan work, there is evidence that teachers understand the importance of feedback. Teachers post first drafts on bulletin boards inside and outside of the classroom and media center. On and around the writing are positive comments written on sticky notes. In student writing folders or notebooks, students have revision and editing checklists that will be used throughout the process.

Interactive Technology

Some of us are old enough to remember a time before sticky notes, word processing, and even electric typewriters. Technology has changed how many writers move through the process. Technology has also given teachers and library media specialists a wider array of options for feedback.

Just as teachers make side comments in the margins on a writer's paper, word processing applications can be used to make comments by formatting the draft into two columns: a larger column for the draft and a narrower column for the comments. In this way the piece can be sent back and forth electronically to receive comments and suggestions for revision or editing. Several word processing applications have sophisticated options to allow the writer and reader to interact. For example, Microsoft Word has a Commenting tool that allows the reader to mark text and make comments throughout the text. The writer can see these comments at the point of use when he hovers over the "red flag" with the cursor. Comments can also be printed out.

In writing this book, the authors began by conversing back and forth in the prewriting stage by sending e-mails about the scope and focus of the book. The early drafts were sent to each other for contributions and feedback. There was even a discussion about placing our manuscript on a Web log or blog to facilitate the collaboration with and feedback to one another. About that time Carl learned of wikis, a type of Web site that allows users to add, remove, or otherwise edit all content very quickly and easily. This newer technology allowed us to track changes, as in the past, but provided greater options for giving feedback. In addition, when we revised or commented on each other's ideas, each member of the team received an e-mail notification automatically.

Blogs and wikis are examples of instant publication. Depending on how quickly a student is working, there can be little time for feedback. It will be important that we work with students in these new formats to enhance reader feedback and not move to publication before quality has been accomplished. There may be other technologies that have emerged since we wrote this book. As library media specialists, we can continue to be on the forefront of seeing how these tools can help our students be better writers by giving them constructive feedback throughout the process.

Formal Evaluation

Assessment of student writing is common in most states and many school corporations. With few exceptions, the students are given a topic with specific information to be included in the sample. This prompted writing provides a common sample across learners to assess the overall program effectiveness. Students are scored on the content (five of the six traits) and conventions (trait six). Typically the library media specialist is not involved in the administration or scoring, but should be informed on the criteria and the modes of writing so that resources can be organized to support greater teacher and student understanding.

Our discussion of writing evaluation will be limited to the products that students produce in the course of their class and course work. Evaluation of writing occurs for several reasons: to determine whether or not a student has accomplished a given goal, to assess the degree to which a product is acceptable in light of specified criteria, and to make instructional adjustments in light of student progress toward expectations. Rubrics and anchor papers are the most common tools for formal evaluation. In the evaluation of writing several interested parties can and should be involved: the writer, teacher, and library media specialist.

Student Self-Evaluation

Self-evaluation can begin easily in conversations with students by asking them to read a sentence or segment that illustrates a skill or trait that has been taught. As students at all grade levels progress in their understanding of the qualities of effective writing, their role can expand to encompass formal evaluation. Students may be asked to select three papers from their writing notebook or portfolio and rank order them by highlighting specific criteria on a checklist for content and conventions. They may also be asked to write summary comments about strengths and weaknesses.

Self-evaluation may occur at any point during the process. Responses to formal criteria with examples that support the judgment are essential qualities of thoughtful evaluation Self-evaluation can occur before or after that of the teacher and library media specialist. Self-evaluation is immensely valuable when students have been taught the criteria and can recognize it in their own writing.

Educator Evaluation

The teachers and library media specialists should use the same criteria as the students, but theirs may be more comprehensive. Decide together what role the library media specialist will have in formal evaluation. Some teachers will be eager for your assistance and others may feel it is their sole domain. Perhaps the best idea is to begin small and focus in on those pieces and parts of the project in which the library media specialist leads the instruction or application. For example, perhaps the LMS could grade the prewriting (research or graphic organizers) to see if students followed the research model, took good notes, organized them thoughtfully, etc. Another option is to assess the sources cited in the final project. It is good not only to assess that students are successfully citing the sources, but also, from a collection development viewpoint, the assessment can help to determine areas of the collection that need updating or need additional copies ordered of a well-used source. Another option is to evaluate the work together. Perhaps during the students' presentations, both the classroom teacher and the library media specialist are using rubrics to score the project and compare notes to arrive at the final score. The criteria may need to be expanded from six traits to adding one more, presentation.

Taking time to self-reflect can help the writer make changes during their next jaunt through the writing process and hopefully improve their writing. Students in second grade and up may even use the rubrics that were given to them at the start of the project to self-assess their project before their teachers. Self-reflection can be very valuable, but it is certainly a skill that needs to be taught and modeled. Many students will often answer questions about what they could have improved on with "nothing" or "everything." Try to share with them that it is important to think much more detailed. "I could have spent more time researching. I could have asked my friend to help edit for fragments." The more specific they are, the more their writing will improve the next time.

One More Thing...

Writing is a recursive process that begins with one or more ideas from the writer and evolves into a product that is shared with an audience. Good writers draw on their own lives for topics to write about and publish for people within and outside of their immediate world. Students can learn how to use the process well when the professionals in a building collaborate. The library media specialist can play a vital role in supporting students and their teachers with the best information, resources, and examples of the type of writing students are learning to create. Effective writing ability is a central element of today's achievement-oriented focus. The library media specialist that understands the why and how to support student writing ability makes an important and critical contribution to the school mission of improved student achievement.

Works Consulted

Murray, Donald. *The Craft of Revision*. Belmont, CA: Thomson Wadsworth, 2004.

Glossary of Terms

active voice verbs
    active voice verbs "show," while passive voice "tells"

anchor papers
    samples of student writing that display the qualities and characteristics that teachers expect students to achieve through their teaching

collaboration
    working together to accomplish common goals

conventions
    the accepted norms and rules for written language that includes spelling, mechanics (punctuation), and usage (grammar)

drafting
    getting ideas down by any means from pencil and paper to electronic so that the writer's ideas can be read by the writer and others

editing
    reviewing and changing a draft to adhere to standard language conventions that include spelling, punctuation, and grammar

focus lesson
    a brief sequence of instruction with one clear teaching point that shows a writer how to improve their writing or solve a problem

invented spelling
    during drafting, students spell a word as it sounds so that they can keep their focus on communication

modes of writing
    the style or structure of the writing that conforms to the purpose for writing: narrative, expository, or persuasive

prewriting
> planning that a writer does in advance of drafting that may include brainstorming ideas, collecting information, interviews, and the making of lists and notes to begin deciding on the topic, audience, purpose, and focus of the writing.

publishing
> concluding the writing process by making the finished piece of writing available to its audience

reciprocal relationship
> a mutually beneficial connection between two factors; reading enhances writing ability and writing benefits reading comprehension

revision
> the stage where writers rework their piece to make their ideas and information clearer and more meaningful to the reader

traits
> characteristics of writing that contribute to its overall quality: ideas, organization, fluency, voice, word choice, and conventions

writing process
> the steps taken to move from ideas within the writer's mind to a finished piece that is published on paper or some other form of media for the intended audience

writing strategies
> plans and techniques the writer uses during the process to accomplish the overall goal of writing or to solve problems

Index

6

6 Traits, 24

A

achievement, 14, 20, 21, 22, 35, 44, 116
anchor papers, 18, 47, 68, 72, 81, 114
assessment, 11, 15, 21, 31, 32, 33, 36, 49, 50, 60, 61, 62, 63, 69, 72, 73, 74, 75, 76, 83, 84, 85, 86, 96, 97, 98, 99, 106, 107, 108, 109, 114, 115,
audience, 13, 14, 15, 17, 23, 24, 25, 26, 27, 28, 29, 31, 32, 33, 34, 37, 38, 41, 45, 49, 52, 53, 56, 58, 65, 66, 71, 77, 78, 80, 83, 85, 101, 102, 103, 104, 107, 108, 109, 111, 112, 113, 116, 118

B

beginnings, 47, 84
blogs, 45, 114

C

citing sources, 56, 91, 103,
collaboration, 10, 15, 43, 44, 45, 46, 48, 60, 61, 62, 63, 73, 74, 75, 76, 83, 84, 85, 86, 96, 97, 98, 99, 103, 106, 107, 108, 109, 114, 117
conferences, 18, 80, 113,
content areas, 11, 22, 86, 108
conventions, 14, 15, 17, 24, 28, 33, 87, 88, 114, 115, 117, 118

D

details, 15, 17, 23, 31, 35, 52, 53, 58, 68, 69, 74, 82, 83, 91, 92
draft, 13, 14, 15, 16, 17, 19, 23, 24, 25, 26, 27, 28, 29, 31, 32, 33, 34, 38, 53, 58, 65, 66, 67, 68, 69, 71, 76, 77, 78, 79, 80, 81, 83, 87, 96, 102, 112, 113, 114, 117, 118

E

edit, 11, 13, 14, 15, 16, 17, 18, 20, 23, 24, 25, 26, 27, 32, 33, 34, 40, 65, 77, 79, 87, 88, 90, 91, 92, 98, 102, 106, 107, 108, 109, 112, 113, 114, 115, 117
evaluation, 11, 16, 18, 44, 45, 46, 54, 60, 61, 62, 63, 73, 74, 75, 76, 83, 84, 85, 86, 96, 97, 98, 99, 102, 106, 107, 108, 109, 111, 114, 115,

F

feedback, 13, 15, 18, 19, 20, 28, 34, 78, 101, 111, 112, 113, 114,
fluency, 16, 24, 118
focus lessons, 17, 81, 113
formal evaluation, 111, 114, 115,

G

genres, 17, 21, 69,

I

ideas, 10, 18, 19, 20, 23, 24, 25, 26, 27, 28, 29, 30, 31, 33, 34, 35, 37, 39, 41, 44, 45, 50, 51, 53, 56, 60, 62, 65, 66, 69, 71, 77, 79, 80, 81, 82, 91, 92, 101, 102, 103, 104, 106, 114, 116, 117, 118
Internet 46, 51, 79, 88, 90, 102, 103

L

Literature Connections, 11, 58, 71, 90, 92, 97, 104

M

Microsoft Word, 79, 114
modes of writing 17, 30, 68, 79, 114, 117

N

narrative writing, 17, 28, 67

O

organization, 13, 17, 24, 25, 28, 29, 39, 49, 50, 53, 56, 58, 63, 68, 69, 70, 75, 80, 112, 118

P

peer feedback, 15, 18,
poetry, 28, 30, 57, 58, 102
prewrite, 14, 17, 24, 25, 27, 31, 34, 37, 49, 51, 52, 53, 65, 66, 101, 102, 113
process approach, 13, 14, 15, 19, 20, 22
product approach, 13, 14, 15,
publish, 14, 15, 24, 27, 28, 33, 34, 41, 45, 79, 81, 87, 101, 102, 103, 104, 113, 116, 118
purposes for writing, 24, 27

R

recursive process, 71, 116
response to writing, 21, 111
revise, 14, 15, 19, 24, 26, 27, 34, 39, 49, 53, 65, 77, 78, 81, 83, 84, 86, 96, 102, 106, 107, 109, 112, 114,

S

student ownership, 16,

V

voice, 16, 24, 25, 39, 49, 58, 85, 90, 91, 98, 108, 112, 117, 118

W

word choice, 24, 39, 58, 88, 89, 118
Works Consulted, 21, 35, 47, 48, 59, 68, 72, 79, 82, 87, 88, 89, 90, 91, 94, 103, 105, 116,
writing process, 10, 11, 13, 14, 15, 16, 19, 23, 24, 27, 28, 29, 34, 35, 43, 45, 49, 58, 77, 79, 87, 88, 92, 101, 102, 103, 112, 113, 115, 118

www.ingramcontent.com/pod-product-compliance
Lightning Source LLC
Chambersburg PA
CBHW080413300426
44113CB00015B/2504